Intimacy with Christ

A 90 Day Journey

By

Lisa M. Black

Lisa M. Black has been teaching the word of God for over twenty years. Her simple and real life way of explaining biblical truths have inspired many to fall in love with the word of God and to live life by God's word. She is the founder of Transforming Life Changing Ministries, which conducts various outreach initiatives throughout the year, including Feed the Need, Back 2 School, and the annual Message of Hope Conference in Ontario, CA. Lisa is the author of the weekly online teaching word, WTLC (Word of God is Transforming, Life Changing), and is the co-host of the weekly radio teaching and encouraging broadcast '*iLive*.' Visit www.KPRO1570.com to listen to the broadcast.

Lisa is a licensed minister, conference speaker, and mentor starting her ministry reaching out to teenage girls through GEMS (God's Emeralds Manifesting His Son), planting seeds of the knowledge of God's love for them. Lisa has an undergraduate degree from Indiana Tech University, a diploma from Vision International, and a bachelor's degree in Theology from Life Christian University. Lisa serves as a facilitator at Abundant Living Bible College in Rancho Cucamonga, California, and serves as an advisory board member to various ministries and organizations.

Lisa has the mandate to fulfill God's purpose for her life; she believes that it is never too late. As an advocate of teaching sound biblical truth, her passion is to see people grasp the depth of God's love. She is strongly convinced that through the Word of God lives are amazingly transformed. Giving all glory to God for all that He has done and allowed her to accomplish, her greatest achievement is being a wife and mother of two. She and her family reside in Southern California.

In Appreciation...

To my King, my Savior, Jesus Christ, I thank you for my intimate walk with you and for your unyielding grace and mercy towards me. Thank you for leading me when I didn't believe in myself, discovering that I only needed to believe in **You**. Thank you for instilling in me your Word and showing me that, "I can do all things through Christ which strengthens me" (Philippians 4: 13).

To my husband George, my covering, who loves, believes, encourages, and supports me constantly to pursue the call of God on my life. I love you, honey. To my children Symone and Malik, the Lord gave you to me and by His power He taught me to be a godly mother and you made it easy. My love for you both is beyond measure. What a joy it was to know that the Lord chose me to carry you both; as He gave you to me; I gave you back to Him.

To my brothers, Chester, Pastor Jeffrey, and Kevin, thank you for always supporting, loving, and watching over me.

To family and friends that extend from east coast to west coast, thank you.

A special thanks to all of my mentors Pastor Jeffrey Brown, Sr., Pastor Jeffrey A. Johnson, Sr., Pastor Michael Bryant, Pastor Tamala Kelly, and Pastor Sharon Takaha thank you for your leadership and for encouraging me to fulfill the call of God on my life.

I pray that these words inspire and draw you to a closer walk with the Savior, Jesus Christ.

INTIMACY with CHRIST A 90 DAY JOURNEY

To contact the author:

Lisa M. Black

P. O. Box 4739

Ontario, CA 91761-4739

TransformingLifeChanging@gmail.com

http://TransformingLifeChanging.org

PREFACE

This book is an expression of a lifetime journey of searching to finally come to the knowledge and understanding of the close relationship and privilege with God, the Father that we have through His Son, Jesus. I truly can say that the God of the universe, the Creator of All things is real and He desires to have a relationship with you. You can believe that you too can have communication and fellowship with Him, through His Son Jesus Christ. Finding God is not difficult, Jesus said, "Ask and it will be given to you; seek and you will find; knock and the door will be opened to you. For everyone who asks receives; he who seeks finds; and to him who knocks, the door will be opened." Matthew 7: 7-8. If you seek Him, you will find Him.

I believe that the barrier that believers face in not hearing God or having the continual communion with Him is the lack of knowledge of His Word. We come to know Jesus intimately through prayer and through His Word. Having an intimate relationship is a knowing, a revelation of close fellowship with God, and an inner knowing of that no matter what may happen God is with you and loves you. *Intimacy with Christ A 90 Day Journey* will take you on a daily path of having close fellowship with the Father. As you read the scripture and meditate on His word you will experience intimacy like never before. My prayer is that you too will enjoy God's presence as you encounter Him every day.

You're Worth More Than You Think

"The thief comes only to steal and kill and destroy; I have come that they may have life, and have it to the full" John 10:10

Now that we celebrate Jesus' resurrection every day and tend to go back to business as usual, don't think that the enemy is going to be silent. On the contrary, he will continue to try to rob you and me of our joy and our peace. He will tell you things such as "You're not worthy, you can't do it, and it will never happen." Remember, he is a liar. In fact it says in John 8:44, *"You belong to your father, the devil, and you want to carry out your father's desire. He was a murderer from the beginning, not holding to the truth, for there is no truth in him. When he lies, he speaks his native language, for he is a liar and the father of lies."* The enemy knows our weaknesses and will prey on us when we are most vulnerable and tired. Be on guard. Don't listen to anything that he says, totally ignore him.

Remember, *Charlie Brown's* teacher, how her voice reflected a tone of a nuisance? After, listening to her for so long, her voice began to sound like "womp, womp, womp." We must have the same attitude of *Charlie Brown* and let the enemy's voice become simply noise and not listen. I love John 10:10. It puts things in the right perspective; Christ died so that we can live eternally with Him, but also to have a full life here on earth. The journey doesn't have to be rough; rather it can be an enjoyable ride when we get on the Lord's agenda and begin to listen to Him and speak his word, instead of agreeing with the enemy.

Your Work Will Be Rewarded

"Then Asa called to the LORD his God and said, "LORD, there is no one like you to help the powerless against the mighty. Help us, O LORD our God, for we rely on you, and in your name we have come against this vast army. O LORD, you are our God; do not let man prevail against this vast army. O LORD, you are our God; do not let man prevail against you. The LORD struck down the Cushites before Asa and Judah. But as for you, be strong and do not give up, for your work will be rewarded." 2 Chronicles 14: 11-12, 15: 7

King Asa was up against a vast army, outnumbered, and out-powered. He did the only thing that he knew to do...he went to God. After God gave him the victory, the prophet's son Azariah warned him about remaining true to God. Beloved, when you feel over-powered by someone or something go to the only source that can help you, and that source is only God. He may use someone to bring what you need to you, but the first step is to be humble and go to Him. Acknowledge that whatever you're facing is too big for you to handle. It may be too big for you, but it is never too big for God.

It is easy to want to give up, to throw in the towel, but instead of giving up give it up to the Lord. Find rest and peace in Him. Stop wrestling and struggling with it, simply surrender whatever it is to the One Who can solve it and direct you. Remember, the Lord sees all your works and He will reward you; nothing goes unnoticed by Him.

Your New Name

"Simon, Simon, Satan has asked to sift you as wheat. But, I have prayed for you Simon that your faith may not fail. And, when you have turned back, strengthen your brothers." Luke 22: 31-32

This disciple failed many times; at this particular time Jesus calls him Simon, referring to his old nature. But, later Jesus gives him the new name of Peter, which speaks of his destiny. When the Lord forgives, He remembers ours sins no more (Isaiah 43: 25) and He gives us new names like, righteousness, fearfully and wonderfully made. He reaches out His hand of acceptance in the same way as He did Peter, and says, come on. His hand says, "I love you," "There is room in my house," "I have work for you to do." Like Peter, the enemy wants to sift us too; he wants to see if we are like the chaff, which blows away with the wind.

Beloved, when the enemy fires a dart at you, dust yourself off and keep it pushing. Don't wallow in self-pity or defeat. When faced with a trial, do you run scared or do you take your stand in the power of the Holy Spirit and use all of the spiritual weapons (Ephesians 6: 10-18) that have been given to you? You are an overcomer in Christ Jesus. Encourage yourself in the Lord, take a hold of His hand and stand.

You Were Created...

"The God said, "Let us make man in our image, in our likeness, and let them rule over the fish of the sea and the birds of the air, over the livestock, over all the earth, and over all the creatures that move along the ground." So God created man in His own image, in the image of God He created them. God blessed them and said to them, "Be fruitful and increase in number; fill the earth and subdue it. Rule over the fish of the sea and the birds of the air and over every living creature that moves on the ground." Genesis 1: 26-28

The passage of scripture confirms and also reminds me that we were created for a purpose. Everything that God created has a purpose. There are no accidents or mishaps; even if the timing seems wrong to us God still has a purpose. Vegetation and animals were created for food for us; the sun, moon, and stars were created to govern the day and the night and to mark seasons, days, and years. We all were created to do something, and God is not confused about anything, nor is He confused about the reason we were created. God knew you and me before we were formed in our mother's womb (Jeremiah 1: 5).

Sometimes it takes years to discover why you were created, but it may not take long if you ask the Creator...something to think about.

Works

"All of us have become like one who is unclean, and all our righteous acts are like filthy rags; we all shrivel up like a leaf, and like the wind our sins sweep us away." Isaiah 64: 6

I'm reminded of this text simply because, even on our most holy day, we are all like filthy rags without the saving power of Jesus. You know we are not saved by our own efforts; we could never work enough to merit eternal life. Humanitarian efforts and good deeds are great and are most needed. However, those works will not get anyone entrance into heaven.

No one can ever stand before God Almighty and say, "I did this or that" with motives of gaining a ticket in, because none of us are worthy to stand before God without Jesus. There is no ticket. Isaiah describes Christ's suffering on the cross, "Just as there were many who were appalled at Him, his appearance was so disfigured beyond human likeness…" (Isaiah 53: 14)

Relax, the work has already been done and I'm glad. I don't have to worry about whether I am working hard enough, because eventually I'm going to mess up (and you will too). I'm so glad that salvation is not predicated on if *I get it right*. Why? The blood covers me and you. *"But He was pierced for our transgressions, He was crushed for our iniquities; the punishment that brought us peace was upon Him, and by His wounds we are healed." Isaiah 53: 5*

Who Do You Say He Is?

"When Jesus came to the region of Caesarea Philippi, He asked His disciples, "Who do people say the Son of Man is?" They replied, "Some say John the Baptist; others say Elijah; and still others, Jeremiah or one of the prophets." "But what about you?" He asked. "Who do you say I am?" Simon Peter answered, "You are the Christ, the Son of the living God." Jesus replied, "Blessed are you, Simon son of Jonah, for this was not revealed to you by man, but by my Father in heaven." Matthew 16: 13-17

The Jews knew that the Messiah had been foretold by the prophets' centuries before; they knew that He would be a descendant of David. However, when He came they did not recognize Him. Although Jesus did miracle, after miracle, they still did not believe. Does this sound familiar? It all goes back to simple belief. I must stay here, because some still don't know Who He is. How many miracles must He do before you believe and trust Him?

Beloved, victory will not be ours if we do not recognize Who Jesus is. We can't be religious like the Pharisees by going to church Sunday after Sunday, year after year, and never know Who He is. Christ was 100% man and at the same time 100% Divine. God manifested himself in the flesh (John 1: 14), the Son of God, Jesus Christ. He came so that we could live with Him for eternity, and to have a personal relationship with Him on earth. All past practices and ceremonies were all foreshadows of Christ's coming. Is He a prophet or a teacher to you, someone that you only seek when in need or someone that mother or grandmother talked about? Who do you say He is?

When God Says No

"Going a little farther, He fell with His face to the ground and prayed, "My Father, if it is possible, may this cup be taken from me. Yet not as I will, but as you will." Matthew 26: 39

The process of growing in our faith includes answers that we may not want to hear...no, or not now. We all want yes; we all want our way. The Lord's answer is exactly what it is. His, "no," isn't maybe, it's no. When we hear, "no," how often do we decide in our minds to do it anyway, and say He really didn't mean no. But what happens, when God says no? Do we complain, murmur, or fall away? Do we have pity parties and walk around depressed with bad attitudes, and do it anyway. I think that we can look to our Lord, Who in spite of the pain He was about to endure said, "Yet not as I will, but as you will." Jesus submitted to the Father.

Beloved, an indication that you are growing in your walk, is the ability to submit to the Father allowing His will to be done. I have to remind myself, "Lisa, you don't know everything; the Lord's way is the only way." Even when we don't understand, we can rest assure that it will work out for our good. Our Father is omnipotent (all powerful), omnipresent (everywhere at all times), and omniscient (all knowing and all seeing). The Lord sees the beginning, middle, and the end. He knows how things will turn out. He knows what we need and what it will take to get us to where we need to be. What is He doing, He is shaping us, conforming us to the image of His Son (Romans 8: 29). We have to learn how to put our total trust and faith in Him, and give our will to Him; for He and He alone knows all things. He has our best interest in His hands, and though it may not feel good, He is working it out for our good.

We Have The Greater One

"You dear children, are from God and have overcome them, because the One Who is in you is greater than the one who is in the world." 1 John 4:4

John's letter to the church is short and brief, yet direct and powerful. It is a warning for believers everywhere to remember what they have always believed, and that is Jesus was and is God in the flesh. He is also telling them to remember that God is love and that there is no darkness in Him. John was an eyewitness to the life, death, resurrection, and ascension of Jesus. He had firsthand experience walking with the Savior.

During the time that 1 John was written, false teachers had infiltrated the church causing the believers to waiver in their beliefs. They taught such things as, it was okay to have fellowship with God and still walk in darkness (vs. 6). That is a lie, no truth is in it. Unfortunately, the same lie is in circulation today. We can't go to church on Sunday, get our praise on, then Monday-Saturday do whatever we want to do. The devil is a liar (John 8: 44). It is time out for that. How can we win the world for Christ, if we, the body of Christ (believers) are doing some of the same things that the world is doing? Don't be a stumbling block for someone else (1 Corinthian 10: 32).

Beloved, I will be the first to admit that this walk is not easy; my flesh wants to act up just like anybody else's. However, the Lord reminds me that He is greater than the one in the world. God has given us the power to overcome the temptations and worldly desires. How? I'm glad you asked. He gave us His Spirit; the Holy Spirit dwells in us and enables us to do all things. Abstain from temptations that are pulling you away; don't live there, run! You can overcome it; Jesus said that we can. Father, help us to cling more to you than to our own desires. Give us a hunger and thirst for you each and every day.

Turn

"Then the LORD your GOD will make you prosperous in all the work of your hands and in the fruit of your womb, the young of your livestock and the crops of your land. The LORD will again delight in you and make you prosperous, just as He delighted in your fathers, if you obey the LORD your God and keep His commands and decrees that are written in this Book of the Law and turn to the LORD your God with all your heart and with all your soul." Deuteronomy 30: 9-10

We, like Israel from time to time need reminders of what God has said. We too can find ourselves so entangled with our own concerns or we get comfortable with our blessings, and fall into traps that lead us out of the will of God. We have modern day idols such as cell phones, social media, television, etc. Please don't misunderstand. These tools are useful, but they should not to take the majority of our attention.

Israel had succumbed to the idolatrous practices of the surrounding nations. They murmured, complained, and indulged in various sinful activities. Moses' plea to get them to turn was simple and direct. His message still applies today...obey and turn. We are living in the last days and the answer to world problems is not in one man or group, but is simply to turn back to God.

Father, forgive us for looking more to the blessings, rather than you the One who has blessed us. Help us to live a more balance life.

True Freedom

"May your unfailing love come to me, O LORD, your salvation according to your promise; then I will answer the one who taunts me, for I trust in your word. Do not snatch the word of truth from my mouth, for I have put my hope in your laws. I will always obey your law, forever and ever. I will walk about in freedom, for I have sought out your precepts. I will speak of your statues before kings and will not be put to shame." Psalm 119: 41-46

David was a man after God's own heart (1 Samuel 13: 14). David loved the Lord and he loved His precepts, His word. He speaks of his confidence in the Lord's promises that when the "One who taunts," that's the enemy, who comes or speaks his lies, his response is, "I trust in Your Word." Do not let the enemy snatch the word from your heart or from your mouth. Jesus teaches us in the parable of the 4 soils in Matthew 13: 18-19,"that when people hear the word, and do not understand it, the enemy comes and snatches away what has been sown in his heart. This is the seed sown along the path." Jesus said in John 10:10, "The thief comes to steal, kill, and destroy; I have come that they may have life, and have it to the full."

Do you hear the progression...steal, kill, and ultimately...destroy? He doesn't play fair; he is a snake, a rascal. We must stay alert at all times. But, the Lord didn't leave us in the hands of the enemy, in the 'b' portion of that verse, Jesus said, "But I have come that you may have life and have it to the full."

Beloved, true freedom is living by the word. Sin binds, but His word sets us free. When we read the word, at first, it is head knowledge; it will take reading it two or three times to read it before it becomes revelation. We have to have an open heart to receive. If we read it from our minds, our intellect, it can be hard to conceive. Through knowing the Lord by the Word, you will know His will.

This Too Shall Pass

"But now, this is what the LORD says, He who created you O Jacob, He who formed you, O Israel," "Fear not, for I have redeemed you; I have summoned you by name; you are mine. When you pass through the waters, I will be with you; and when you pass through the rivers, they will not sweep over you. When you walk through the fire, you will not be burned; the flames will not set you ablaze, for I am the LORD, your God, the Holy One of Israel, your Savior." Isaiah43:

I love this passage. Take note of the key word...pass. It is important to understand that though the situation you're in may be difficult and challenging, it will soon pass. Our circumstances won't stay the same. Take a look back at last year and the year before. If He brought you through that, He can bring you through this. Don't believe the lie that it is forever. Nothing is forever, only eternity with God. No matter what is going on the Lord is with you (Hebrews 13: 5). Although heaven may appear or seem like brass, as if there is no connection when you call, please rest assured the Lord hears and sees everything. Does the Lord blow the storm in our direction? Possibly or He allows it. However the case, He is with us. Dare we ask, "What can I learn from this, or have I been enrolled (unknowingly) in the class...Character Building 101?

Beloved, when you don't know what to do or you're anxious about what or when to do, relax and simply trust God. He is faithful.

The Word Became Flesh

"The Word became flesh and made His dwelling among us. We have seen His Glory, the Glory of the One and Only, Who came from the Father, full of grace and truth." John 1: 14

Jesus is the Word; He is the Alpha and Omega, the Beginning and the End. God said, "Let Us make man in Our image, in Our likeness..." (Genesis 1: 26) After the fall, God said to the serpent, "And I will put enmity between you and the woman, and between your offspring and hers; He will crush your head, and you will strike His heel." (Genesis 3: 15) What God said to the serpent is so powerful; it shows His grace and love for us, in that, though man failed, God never would fail.

Through Satan's attempt to thwart God's plan and the crucifixion, "He will crush your head," foreshadows Christ's victory and Satan's defeat through the resurrection. (LASB) Hallelujah! So we know that Jesus is, was, and is still to come. He was at the beginning and will be at the end. He is forever, eternal.

Beloved, Jesus is not far away into the heavens that He cannot identify with your pain or situation. He was faced with all conditions that we face and tempted by the enemy, yet He was without sin. Don't think that He does not care about you, or what is going on in your life...He cares. He cared enough to come down to earth to see about you, me, and the whole world. And, though He is at the Right Hand of the Father, His Spirit lives in us. He is still very much with us. Praise His Name.

The Untouchables

"So the king gave the order, and they brought Daniel and threw him into the lion's den. The king said to Daniel, "May your God, Whom you serve continually rescue you!"...At the first light of dawn, the king got up and hurried to the lion's den. When he came near the den, he called do Daniel in an anguished voice, "Daniel, servant of the living God, has your God, Whom you serve continually, been able to rescue you from the lions?" Daniel answered, "O king, live forever! My God sent His angel and He shut the mouths of the lions. They have not hurt me, because I was found innocent in His sight. Nor have I ever done any wrong before you, O king." Daniel 6: 16, 19-22

Did you know that the enemy can't touch you unless he gets permission from God (Job 1 and 2)? This story of Daniel depicts God's sovereignty, protection, and His power. The One who created the lion has the same power to shut the lion's mouth. That's good news to me.

Daniel is one of my favorite people in the bible. He was a man of integrity and a man devoted to God. He did not allow the pressures of society stop him or sway him to disobey...he remained true, faithful, and obedient. Daniel is one of many who like the superheroes, the Untouchables, used his super power, The Lord, to protect him.

Beloved, you also have the super power of God Who protects and watches over you and yours. In spite of anything that the enemy, or any opposition that comes against you, trust in your God to deliver you.

The Thing to Do Is Pray

"If My people, who are called by My name, will humble themselves and pray and seek My face and turn from their wicked ways, then will I hear from heaven and will forgive their sin and will heal their land." 2 Chronicles 7: 14

One of the main themes of 2 Chronicles is the building of the temple by Solomon, the son of David and it parallels 1 and 2 Kings. It also highlights the reign of the kings of Judah, good and bad, and 2 Chronicles 7:14 is the key verse of the book. The Lord gave this command to Solomon after he had finished the temple commanding him to inform the people that their ability to hear from God was predicated on their commitment to walk in the commands of God and to observe His laws and decrees.

I recently had a conversation with an individual about the unemployment rate in America, and during the conversation my spirit became grieved about the number of people who are out of work, especially the people of God. My first thought was, "Who is praying and why not?" Not only should we pray about our own personal needs, but we should be praying about the needs of people worldwide. We are commanded to pray for our government officials as well, *"I urge, then, first of all, that requests, prayers, intercession and thanksgiving be made for everyone-for kings and all those in authority, that we may live peaceful and quiet lives in all godliness and holiness 1 Timothy 2:2."*

Beloved, as we humble ourselves, pray, and turn from sin God promises to hear us and He will heal our land. There is so much wickedness around us; let's not take the approach of talking about how bad things are, how bad our young people are acting, or how high gas and food prices are, instead pray and pray without ceasing. God will hear our prayers and bring about a change in the earth. We have the privilege and the power, let's use it. To God Be The Glory!

The Box

"The Egyptians...all Pharaoh's horses, chariots, horsemen, and troops pursued the Israelites and overtook them as they camped by the sea near Pi Hahiroth, opposite Baal Zephon. As Pharaoh approached, the Israelites looked up and there were the Egyptians, marching after them. They were terrified and cried out to the LORD. They said to Moses, "Was it because there were no graves in Egypt that you brought us to the desert to die? What have you done to us by bringing us out of Egypt? Didn't we say to you in Egypt, "Leave us alone; let us serve the Egyptians"? It would have been better for us to serve the Egyptians than to die in the desert!"

Moses answered the people, "Do not be afraid. Stand firm and you will see the deliverance the LORD will bring you today. The Egyptians you see today you will never see again. The LORD will fight for you; you need only to be still." Exodus 14: 9-14

I've never like mazes. Why, because, the times that I have been in one I felt trapped and lost with no way out. Israel was trapped between Pharaoh and his army, and the Red sea...a familiar story that we all know, but one that can serve as a reminder. Have you ever felt trapped? Have you ever turned to the left and there was a wall, then to only turn to the right and run into another wall? I was recently in a situation with walls all around me. Deep within my spirit the Lord showed me a box with the lid open. I thought about that box and wondered what I would do if I was in the box, and to my amazement He told me to look up. Beloved, whenever you find yourself walled in on every side look up. Look to the One Who can pull you out.

The Purpose of Prayer

"Do not be anxious about anything, but in everything, by prayer and petition, with thanksgiving, present your requests to God. And the peace of God, which transcends all understanding, will guard your hearts and your minds in Christ Jesus." Philippians 4: 6-7

Prayer is a privilege. Why pray? Prayer is the ability to release our burdens and to give the Lord full reign in that situation. It is literally giving it over to Him. When we pray, we give Him access, or we allow Him to work. We give Him the permission to handle it. We know that God is sovereign and that He knows what's going on, before we pray. But, He desires that intimate fellowship with us and Him. This is one of my favorite verses, and I have to remind myself, when I find myself getting anxious that I can pray about everything; I can take all my concerns to the Lord. I can cast all my burdens on Him, because He cares. And, the best part about this verse is that it says, "And the peace of God..." God will give us peace. He will keep us in perfect peace whose mind is stayed on Him (Isaiah 26: 3).

You can walk away from your prayer with peace, knowing that you have laid down your cares and given them over to God, the Father, the One Who can and will work all things out for the good. It's like going to your mother and father with an issue, and having the assurance that they will take care of it for you. But, if an earthly mother and father will do their best to help in a time of need, our heavenly Father will do even greater things (Luke 11: 11-13). He will give us His best. Beloved, today are you walking in peace or are you worrying about everything. The purpose of prayer is for deliverance, or to satisfy a need, but it is having a peace that surpasses all understanding. Even if you are in a tight place and don't know which way to turn, turn to the Lord in prayer.

The 3 R's

"LORD, who may dwell in your sanctuary? Who may live on your holy hill? He whose walk is blameless and who does what is righteous, who speaks the truth from his heart and has no slander on his tongue, who does his neighbor no wrong and casts no slur on his fellowman, who despises a vile man but honors those who fear the LORD, who keeps his oath even when it hurts, who lends his money without usury and does not accept a bribe against the innocent. He who does these things will never be shaken." Psalm 15: 1-5

What does righteousness mean? I'm glad you asked it means to act in a moral correct manner. Yes, there is a standard that we must keep...holiness. Peter quoted what the Lord said, "For it is written: "Be holy, because I am holy." (1 Peter 1: 16, Leviticus 11: 44) With that being said, we can do it. We can live holy lives; God's power to live holy resides in each of us.

But, you know there is another description of righteousness that will blow your mind...a divine declaration. Through the Lamb that sacrificed His blood we have been ***declared righteous***. Why, because salvation is a free gift and not of works (Ephesians 2: 8-9). I thank God for the saving power of Jesus, His shed blood. I'm sure by now you're wondering what are the 3 R's...**repent, renew, and resolve**. Repent of your sins, renew your mind through the word, and resolve to start anew. Beloved, if you've missed the mark (and we all do), did you know that you can come boldly to the throne of Grace and find mercy and peace (Hebrews 4: 16)? Receive the Lord's forgiveness...it's free (Ephesians 2: 8-9)

The Blood

"In fact, the law requires that nearly everything be cleansed with blood and without the shedding of blood there is no forgiveness." Hebrews 9: 22

My life and mandate is to continually be a student of the word, and I must admit that digging in the Old Testament, the significance of the sacrifices, rituals, and offerings can be difficult to understand. But, I'm committed to know the truth and I hope that you are too. All of the sacrifices and offerings pointed to the ultimate sacrifice of Jesus. He represents the curtain that separated the Holy Place and the Most Holy Place.

When Christ died the curtain in the temple tore from top to bottom (Mark 15: 38), giving us free access to God. We now no longer need to approach God through priests and sacrifices. The blood is our proof, the blood cleanses us, and the blood allows us to stand in the presence of Almighty God. You don't have to feel guilty, confess your sins to God, and come boldly before the throne of Grace. God is ever-present and He is always wanting to commune with you. What an awesome privilege to have a relationship with God the Father through His Son, Jesus. Thank you Jesus, for the blood that you shed on Calvary.

Take it to the Bank

"Every word of God is flawless; He is a shield to those who take refuge in Him." Proverbs 30: 5

I would like to encourage you to spend more time in His word. We have everything accessible at our fingertips; you know we really don't have an excuse. We must fight against focusing on things that do not matter and put our focus back on God. Because, I believe that we are on a journey through 3 stages of life...in the storm, coming out of the storm, or on our way to a storm. But, we can "Be of good cheer, Jesus said, "He has overcome the world (John 16: 33)."

No matter what stage or season you are in, the Word of God is your anchor and sustainer. In this text, the writer, Agur, son of Jakeh was a wise man; he recognizes the infallible word of God; it is flawless. God's word is true, in fact, He is Truth, He is the Spirit of Truth. He is the Word; we can put our trust in Him therefore, we can put our trust in His word. "He is a shield to those who take refuge in Him." A shield is a covering, a defensive armor. A defensive position on the basketball court is a position of defense, the player has to guard the basket, and he prevents the opponent from scoring. God protects us, defends us, and keeps the enemy from scoring.

Beloved, we already have victory through Christ. When the enemy speaks lies to you, and that is all he can do, because Jesus said, "He speaks his own native language. He is the father of lies," John 8: 44. Don't listen to him; take refuge and security in the arms of Jesus, in the security of His Word.

Strength That Can Stand the Test of Time

"But we have this treasure in jars of clay to show that this all-surpassing power is from God and not from us. We are hard pressed on every side, but not crushed; perplexed, but not in despair; persecuted, but not abandoned; struck down, but not destroyed. We always carry around in our body the death of Jesus, so that the life of Jesus may also be revealed in our body. For we who are alive are always being given over to death for Jesus' sake, so that His life may be revealed in our mortal body. So then, death is at work in us, but life is at work in you. Therefore we do not lose heart. Though outwardly we are wasting away, yet inwardly we are being renewed day by day. For our light and momentary troubles are achieving for us an eternal glory that far outweighs them all; so we fix our eyes not on what is seen, but on what is unseen. For what is seen is temporary, but what is unseen in eternal." 2 Corinthians 4: 7-12, 16-18

I look forward to the Olympic Games every four years. One of my favorite events is track and field. It amazes me how the long distant runners are so lean and somewhat frail, yet possess an inner strength that propels them to run such long distances. They have trained their bodies, disciplined themselves in eating nutritional foods, and in turn have the physical ability to keep running without quitting. Our "jars of clay" is perishing, but our inner man is being renewed day by day. The fuel that keeps us running is the "all-surpassing power" that can only come from the Lord.

Beloved, anything that we do is only done through God's power; when you feel tired, over-whelmed, and ready to give up, remember, and go back to the filling station of Jesus to get re-fueled to continue to run your race.

Steak verses Chicken

"The Egyptians...all Pharaoh's horses, chariots, horsemen, and troops pursued the Israelites and overtook them as they camped by the sea near Pi Hahiroth, opposite Baal Zephon. As Pharaoh approached, the Israelites looked up and there were the Egyptians, marching after them. They were terrified and cried out to the LORD. They said to Moses, "Was it because there were no graves in Egypt that you brought us to the desert to die? What have you done to us by bringing us out of Egypt? Didn't we say to you in Egypt, "Leave us alone; let us serve the Egyptians"? It would have been better for us to serve the Egyptians than to die in the desert!" Exodus 14: 9-12

Really...? I've often wanted to ask the Israelites (if I could). Would you really rather have died in Egypt? I believe that the children of Israel suffered from amnesia; they forgot what it was like to be in bondage. They forgot how for years they had cried out to the Lord.

Beloved, change is uncomfortable. In fact, it can be downright unfair (so we sometimes think). But, it is necessary and paramount for our development. Don't fight the process, but embrace it. It is only for a moment...a temporary discomfort that will yield fruit in its season. We all know the old adage, 'no pain...no gain.' And, it definitely doesn't help the process to complain. I have to ask myself this question...Lisa, are you growing? Or, are you still the same. Remember Jesus words in John 15: 1-3, "I am the True Vine, and My Father is the Gardener. He cuts off every branch in Me that bears no fruit, while every branch that does bear fruit He prunes, so that it will be even more fruitful."

Ssh...Listen

"Whether you turn to the right or to the left, your ears will hear a voice behind you, saying, "This is the way; walk in it." Isaiah 30: 21

I love the word of God. Why? It is the voice of God speaking to us; it tells us everything that we need. And, what really is so awesome about it, there is 'nothing new under the sun'. So, whatever you're going through it is not so foreign to God that He can't solve it. If we look closely in the word we will find everything in it to solve all of our problems. It is also wonderful to know that those who lived before us during 'bible days' experienced the same trials and temptations that we experience. We can learn from their mistakes. One problem is that when we don't quiet ourselves and listen and follow God's direction we end up in a mess. This is what Israel was experiencing in this text. They lived in a constant cycle of disobedience and repentance, but God was always there to forgive them and to bless them.

Beloved, when you don't know which way to go simply quiet yourself and listen, God will speak. I know that it is challenging to quiet ourselves; we live on a fast track to where? Who knows... life is just busy these days, but we have to find the time to listen so that we don't end up in a crash on this fast track. Deuteronomy 30: 19-20 states, "This day I call heaven and earth as witnesses against you that I have set before you life and death, blessings and curses. Now choose life, so that you and your children may live and that you may love the LORD your God, **listen to His voice, and hold fast to Him**. For the LORD is your life, and He will give you many years in the land He swore to your fathers, Abraham, Isaac, and Jacob."

Slow Down

"Come to me, all you who are weary and burdened, and I will give you rest. Take my yoke upon you and learn from me, for I am gentle and humble in heart, and you will find rest for your souls. For my yoke is easy and my burden is light." Matthew 11: 28-30

In today's society it's difficult to focus with so many distractions begging for our attention. Driving by is the 'in thing.' Why, because, we've got to get to our next fifty appointments. We drive through our favorite fast food restaurant, we drive through the car wash, and we drive through to get our morning coffee.

Are we also driving through prayer? And, when we stop for that moment are we really giving our cares to the only One Who can solve them, or do we struggle to let them go? Worry causes stress, stress causes sickness, and sickness can cause...(we don't want to go there).

Beloved, Jesus' shoulders are much bigger than ours and capable of carrying anything that we give Him. What's also so great is that He already knows; He's just waiting on you to let it go.

Sheep Qualities

"The LORD is my shepherd, I shall not want. He makes me lie down in green pastures, He leads me beside quiet waters, He restores my soul. He guides me in paths of righteousness for His name's sake. Even though I walk through the valley of the shadow of death, I will fear no evil, for you are with me; your rod and your staff, they comfort me. You prepare a table before me in the presence of my enemies. You anoint my head with oil; my cup overflows. Surely goodness and love will follow me all the days of my life, and I will dwell in the house of the LORD forever." Psalm 23

David, a man after God's own heart loved the Lord; he dedicated his life to worshiping, serving, and honoring God. In this psalm, David is acknowledging the Lord as his Shepherd. He had firsthand knowledge of the qualities of a shepherd, for he spent his early years taking care of sheep, as well as, he understood the characteristics of sheep in that, they are vulnerable, trusting, and not to mention...dirty.

Although, sheep may be looked upon as needy and incapable of caring for themselves, they possess a great quality that in earthly standards is weak and not attractive, and that quality is humility. The humble follow and they understand that there is a greater One who has the answers and that they don't. Beloved, don't try to figure things out yourself...just follow. Which way will you go, your own way or His?

Shake It Off

"Paul gathered a pile of brushwood and, as he put it on the fire, a viper, driven out by the heat, fastened itself on his hand. When the islanders saw the snake hanging from his hand, they said to each other, "This man must be a murderer; for though he escaped from the sea, justice has not allowed him to live." But Paul shook the snake off into the fire and suffered no ill effects. Acts 28: 3-5

In 2012 Manteo Mitchell, Olympic 4x400 runner, ran his race with a broken leg and finished. Many athletes can empathize with Manteo's competitive drive and his determination to finish what he started. The Apostle Paul's assignment was to preach the Gospel to the Gentiles; he had a mission to accomplish, though not a 'mission impossible;' his assignment was not over. He could not let even the bite of a snake distract him from his purpose. The show must go on, parents can you agree? There are no sick days when parenting children; you have to still work, cook, and care for those children. When I injured my Achilles heel I experienced excruciating pain to the point that I had to go to emergency. I had a previously scheduled event, but had to cancel the first session. **But God,** gave me the strength to go, but on crutches, and he healed me. After about a week of discomfort I was totally healed.

Beloved, don't let the bite of unforgiveness, bitterness or offense stop you. Why? The enemy is not trying to get you angry or to just irritate you, on the contrary, he is trying to destroy you, kill your mission, and kill your purpose. Don't let him. Be watchful! Shake it off! Keep it moving. Speak the word of God, His promises over your "light afflictions" so that you may finish your race.

Real Living

"Jesus answered, "It is written, Man does not live on bread alone, but on every word that comes from the mouth of God." Matthew 4: 4

We learn the word, we meditate on it, we memorize it, and we have learned the power of speaking it. We know that life and death are in the power of the tongue (Proverbs 18: 21). We must speak the word of God over our situation. I'd like to pose the question: Has it become life to you. The word of God must become life to us, not an ornament to collect dust, or in today's times, to have it as another app on your phone. Rather, it must become who we are, how we live, it must govern the decisions in which we make. The Word, is God, inspired by the Holy Spirit, written by man (2 Timothy 3: 16, 2 Peter 1: 20-21). The word is our standard and the only standard in which we live as children of God. God is the same, He changes not. He is the same, yesterday, today, and forevermore (Hebrews 13: 8). Nothing going on in your life or mine is new...nothing new under the sun.

My challenge to you today is to let the word become life to you, that's real living, the word of God becoming your life, how you live. We are not to be just hearers of the word, but doers as James tells us. David said in Psalm 119: 11, "I have hidden your word in my heart that I might not sin against you." Jesus in this text, Matthew 4: 4, tells us what to do to fight against temptation. James 4: 7 says, "Submit yourself then to God, resist the devil, and he will flee from you." Joseph was a type of Christ, in that, his purpose, assignment, was to be a deliverer. He resisted the temptation brought on by Potiphar's wife. Whatever you're going through you can resist it. It states in 1 Corinthians 10: 13, "No temptation has seized you except what is common to man. And God is faithful; He will not let you be tempted beyond what you can bear. But, when you are tempted, He will also provide a way out so that you can stand up under it." Real living is a life that is living by the Word of God.

Pure Thoughts

Finally brothers, whatever is true, whatever is noble, whatever is right, whatever is pure, whatever is lovely, whatever is admirable-if anything is excellent or praiseworthy-think about such things." Philippians 4: 8

"Oh, it's not hurting anyone," some say. Maybe you've had this thought or may have uttered these words. The truth is; it is hurting someone, whether it is you or those around you. We may have never wondered why negative or hurtful words come out of our mouth. Old habits can be hard to break. Where do these impure thoughts originate? It's very subtle, but powerful, they originate from that big 50 inch box that we sit in front of, music, those little hand-held or desktop devices, and from our environments...those who are in close proximity. Oh, and of course, they come from within. Be careful and be watchful.

Beloved, pure thoughts produce pure actions. Jesus said, "But the things that come out of the mouth come from the heart, and these make a man unclean. For out of the heart come evil thoughts, murder, adultery, sexual immorality, theft, false testimony, and slander." (Matthew 15: 18-19) Some of you may be saying, "That's just how I am." No...if Christ dwells in you, He has given you the power to overcome. You are a new creation (2 Corinthians 5: 17). Stay close to Him. You know that the more you are around a person, you start acting like them. Stay in the word, and ask Him to change those things that need changing; starting with the heart.

Power of Prayer

"But He said to me, "My grace is sufficient for you, for my power is made perfect in weakness." 2 Corinthians 12: 9

In this text Paul had been given great revelations, and he says, that to keep him from becoming conceited he was given a thorn in the flesh. I would like to talk about through humility, is where the power of prayer comes into play, through giving it all over to God. When we release the reigns and we give it all to Him, in turn, we are acknowledging our weakness, therefore allowing God's strength to prevail. When we do this, God gets the glory, not us. We tend to want to do things on our own, without God. Or, we wait 5 minutes and if the Lord hasn't shown up, we jump in and try to fix it ourselves.

Ask Sara and Abraham. When they were waiting for the promise…Isaac, Sarah became anxious and asked Abraham to have her handmaiden, Hagar lay with him, which caused all kinds of problems (Genesis 16: 2). And that's what happens to us, we encounter more problems when we do things in our own strength, rather in our weakness, by giving it over to God, which is allowing His strength to work things out. "His power is made perfect in weakness."

Beloved, it's time to stop wrestling and struggling. Stop fighting and give it to God, by humbly submitting to Him, so that in your weakness, He is strong; there is no other way. We must understand that the power of prayer is becoming weak, so that He is strong in every situation.

Privilege of Prayer

"The curtain of the temple was torn in two from top to bottom. And when the centurion, who stood there in front of Jesus, heard His cry and saw how He died, he said, "Surely this Man was the Son of God!" Mark 15: 38-39

Today's scripture is one of the most powerful scriptures in the word of God. When Jesus died the curtain (veil) was torn from top to bottom, symbolizing that God opened the way for us to have access to Him (LASB). The very tool, privilege, which sustains, strengthens, and anchors us, is the very thing, or lack of that keeps us wondering, complaining, and worrying. It states in Philippians 4: 6-7, "Do not be anxious about anything, but in **everything (not some things, but everything),** by prayer and petition, with thanksgiving, present your requests to God. And the peace of God, which transcends all understanding, will guard your hearts and your minds in Christ Jesus."

What is prayer? Prayer is immediate access to the Father. God is not far off in the heavens and is distant, that He does not hear our prayers or care. Jesus made it possible for us to come boldly to the throne of grace. We have been given the privilege of prayer, but, how often do we pray. Some may say, why pray? I pray and nothing happens. It says in Daniel 10: 12-13, "...Since the first day that you set your mind to gain understanding and to humble yourself before your God, your words were heard, and I have come in response to them. But the prince of the Persian kingdom resisted me twenty-one days."

It may be that your prayers are being stopped or hindered by other forces. The answer to that is to keep praying. Pray without ceasing. Psalm 34: 17, "The righteous cry out, and the LORD hears them; He delivers them from **all** their troubles. Proverbs 15: 29, "The LORD is far from the wicked, but He hears the prayer of the righteous." Don't stop; don't give up on your situation. God hears your prayers and in His time, He will deliver and work out His perfect will. The privilege of prayer is the key to unlock and to breakdown strongholds. Ephesians 6: 10-18 lists the spiritual weapons that we have been given and they are followed up, or completed by prayer. I encourage you to use one of the greatest gifts that we've been given...prayer, the privilege of prayer.

Peace In The Storm

*"That day when evening came, He said to His disciples, "Let us go over to the other side." Leaving the crowd behind, they took Him along, just as He was, in the boat. There were also other boats with Him. A furious squall came up, and the waves broke over the boat, so that it was nearly swamped. Jesus was in the stern, **sleeping** on a cushion. The disciples woke Him and said to Him, "Teacher, don't you care if we drown?" He got up, rebuked the wind and said to the waves, "Quiet! Be still!" Then the wind died down and it was completely calm. He said to His disciples, "Why are you so afraid? Do you still have no faith?" They were terrified and asked each other, "Who is this? Even the wind and the waves obey Him!" Mark 4: 35-41*

Yes and absolutely, even the winds obey Jesus. I love this story and I have to remind myself to be still. Peace in the storm; what does that look like. I can only imagine Jesus sleeping in the boat, while the hurricane like winds beat against the boat; waves reaching heights over one hundred feet, anything that was once secure is now uprooted, and Jesus sleeps. Does this sound familiar? Have you wondered if Jesus is sleeping while you are going through...? Does it feel as though what was once secure has now become unsecure? **"HAVE FAITH IN GOD."** Mark 11: 22

Beloved, you can rest assured that Jesus is definitely with you during the storm. You can also rest assured that at any moment (His moment) He will tell the wave, "Quiet! Be still!" I love that. That tells me that I don't have to worry; I only need to trust Him. If Jesus is sleeping, shouldn't we also?

Now What?

"Now, that same day two of them were going to a village called Emmaus, about seven miles from Jerusalem. They were talking with each other about everything that had happened. As they talked and discussed these things with each other, Jesus Himself came up and walked along with them; but they were kept from recognizing Him. He asked them, "What are you discussing together as you walk along? They stood still, their faces downcast." Luke 24: 13-17

The greatest story ever told is the story of the life, death, and resurrection of Jesus...a historical event like no other. The resurrection is what validates our faith and what keeps us. There are many religions out there, but only one True God; the resurrection is our proof.

Now what? Now, what do we do post-resurrection? We live because He lives. We are to live the life that He came to earth to give us (John 10:10). Don't go back to yesterday. Don't go back to oppression, depression, lack, and doubt, rather live a life of hope and assurance. Jesus is no longer physically here on earth; He left His Spirit, the Holy Spirit, the Comforter to be with us. Are you wondering around not knowing what to do like the two disciples? Are you still concerned about things that Jesus has already given you victory?

No Cross…No Crown

"As they were going out, they met a man from Cyrene, named Simon, and they forced him to carry the cross. They came to a place called Golgotha (which means the place of the skull)." Matthew 27: 32-33

It was the will of the Father to crush Him (Isaiah 53: 10). He, Jesus, was sent to die so that we can live, live in eternity with Him. His assignment, His purpose wasn't easy, pretty, or comfortable. He paid a heavy price, a price that only He could pay. And, though He took on the form of man (John 1: 14), He was one hundred percent Divine. He is the Only One Who is worthy, the Only One to open the seals (Revelation 5: 2). The One Who has sat down at the right hand of the Father, and this was His assignment and said, "It is finished." Thank you, Jesus.

Did you know that you have a divine assignment? We pray and say, "Lord, use me." Really? I too have said that. We all want to be like our Lord, but to be like Him is to be humble, to humbly submit and obey the Father. It is to endure the pain, the challenge, the difficult circumstance. But, don't beat yourself up when you fail, and just know we all fail. There is none righteous, no not one (Romans 3: 10). We will miss the mark, relax, His grace will cover us. What do you do? Get back up and try it again, again, and again. To be used by God will mean going through the fire. It is a refining process, one that can only come through fire, heat, or that which is difficult and in some cases, unbearable.

But, guess what? Be of good cheer, "Jesus has overcome the world," the same power that raised Christ from the dead lives in us, the believer (Romans 8: 11). Will you carry the cross for Him? Will you take up your cross and follow Him? The end result is pure gold; we will come out as pure gold, being conformed into the image of His Son. That's what it is all about. So, rejoice!!

Not Guilty

"You see, at just the right time, when we were still powerless, Christ died for the ungodly. Very rarely will anyone die for a righteous man, though for a good man someone might possibly dare to die. But God demonstrates His own love for us in this: While we were still sinners, Christ died for us. Since we have now been justified by His blood, how much more shall we be saved from God's wrath through Him! For if, when we were God's enemies, we were reconciled to Him through the death of His Son, how much more, having been reconciled, shall we be saved through His life! Not only is this so, but we also rejoice in God through our Lord Jesus Christ, through whom we have now received reconciliation." Romans 5: 6-11

I cannot imagine what it would feel like to be on death row for a crime that I had committed. Well, at one time (BC...BEFORE CHRIST) we who are saved, were all guilty and sentenced to death (Romans 6: 23), but now we have been pardoned, set free. We don't have to pay the penalty for our sins, why? Christ paid it all for us. I think we need to remind ourselves of the sacrificial price that Jesus paid for us.

You don't have to feel guilty for something that you have been forgiven. You don't have to walk around with shame and guilt for the rest of your life. Of course, we must always confess, and ask for the Lord to forgive us for anything that we do. Because, in this body we will sin...miss the mark. However, we are not condemned. Jesus came not to condemn the world, but to save the world.

Beloved, you've been given a not guilty verdict and now you can go home free. You have a home in heaven awaiting you.

New Wine

"No one sews a patch of unshrunk cloth on an old garment, for the patch will pull away from the garment, making the tear worse. Neither do men pour new wine into old wineskins. If they do, the skins will burst, the wine will run out and the wineskins will be ruined. No, they pour new wine into new wineskins, and both are preserved." Matthew 9: 17

We are in a season of new, fresh, and things never done before and I love it. We must always be looking and expecting the Lord to do new things; with that in mind, we must be ready when God wants to do something new in our life. In this text, Jesus challenges the Pharisees with their strict rules and regulations; He was bringing in something new, though it was prophesied and that new message was reconciliation with God through Him. He didn't come to abolish the law, but to fulfill it.

Beloved, we have to change our mindset; don't always look for Him in the same way. Change is inevitable and change is necessary to grow. We can learn from the old, but we must be ready to embrace the new.

Multiplication

"As evening approached, the disciples came to Him and said, "This is a remote place, and it's already getting late. Send the crowds away, so they can go to the villages and buy themselves some food." Jesus replied, "They do not need to go away. You give them something to eat." "Bring them here to me," He said. And He directed the people to sit down on the grass. Taking the five loaves and the two fish and looking up to heaven, He gave thanks and broke the loaves. Then He gave them to the disciples, and the disciples gave them to the people. They all ate and were satisfied, and the disciples picked up twelve basketfuls of broken pieces that were left over. The number of those who ate was about five thousand men, besides women and children." Matthew 14: 15-21

Math was never my favorite subject. However, we understand that we need to know math for everyday life and to definitely know how to count our money. No, this is not a math lesson. God's multiplication is far above any comprehension; even those with the most brilliant minds that have ever lived cannot compute God's math. When He says, "Go or do," you can rest assure that He will provide and multiply everything that you need. In verse 18, Jesus told the disciples "Bring them here to Me."

Beloved, that's good news to me. Lack does not exist with our God. Whatever you need take it to the Father and ask Him, and watch Him multiply it.

Make Deposits, Not Withdrawals

"How, then, can they call on the One they have not believed in? And how can they believe in the One of Whom they have not heard? And how can they hear without someone preaching to them? And how can they preach unless they are sent? As it is written, "How beautiful are the feet of those who bring good news!" Romans 10: 14-15

"There's a new restaurant in town," or "Macy's is having a 75% off sale," to some this would be good news, ecstatic news. We can't wait to tell somebody about something that has excited us, or that has brought us great joy. Unfortunately, often times gossip and slander is being told rather than the good news of Jesus Christ. When we make deposits, in the natural, at a bank that is great, but at some time we will make a withdrawal and those funds are gone. However, when we make deposits in the Kingdom of God, we are in turn, "*storing up treasures in heaven" (Matthew 6: 19)*.

Let's be on our guard and watchful at all times to always be about our Father's business and share the good news, and not take for granted the opportunities that He gives us daily to tell someone about Him.

Beloved, in today's times it is critical that we are vigilant in sharing the good news. You may be saying, "I don't know what to say, or I'm not a preacher." You don't have to be called to preach, nor do you have to know everything about the bible from Genesis to Revelations right now. Although, it is your responsibility to know the word (2 Timothy 2: 15), but simply telling what the Lord has done for you is a seed planted. Remember, one plants, another waters, and God will give the increase (1 Corinthians 3: 6-7).

Love, No Strings Attached

"Love is patient, love is kind. It does not envy, it does not boast, it is not proud. It is not rude, it is not self-seeking, it is not easily angered, it keeps no record of wrongs. Love does not delight in evil but rejoices with the truth. It always protects, always trusts, always hopes, always perseveres. Love never fails." 1 Corinthians 13: 4-8

The book of 1 Corinthians was written by Paul "to identify problems in the Corinthian church;" problems such as divisions, sexual immorality,and all types of immorality-sound familiar. To this very day some of these same issues plaque the body of Christ, and should not be so. Paul also talks about spiritual gifts; he exhorts the believers in chapter 12 about each of the spiritual gifts.

We all want to make sure that we not only know what are spiritual gifts are, but most assuredly we want to be using our gifts. But, what has been in my spirit lately by the Lord is that it is wonderful to have such gifts, but if they are not accompanied by love they are nothing. (1 Corinthians 13)

Beloved, I don't believe that God is impressed with anything that we do, if it is not done out of a heart of love; not selfishly, not out of compulsion, or out of wanting something in return. Our flesh wants mostly to please itself, and the only way to combat this is to truly get to know how Christ loves. His love is unconditional. Father, help us to love like you love, and help us to not look upon others for what they can do for us, but what we can do for them without any strings attached. *"But God demonstrates His own love for us in this: While we were still sinners, Christ died for us." Romans 5: 8*

Life Father, Like Son

"How great is the love the Father has lavished on us, that we should be called children of God! And that is what we are! The reason the world does not know us is that it did not know Him. Dear friends, now we are children of God, and what we will be has not yet been made known. But we know that when He appears, we shall be like Him, for we shall see Him as He is. Everyone who has this hope in Him purifies himself, just as He is pure. Everyone who sins breaks the law; in fact, sin is lawlessness. But you know that He appeared so that He might take away our sins. And in Him is no sin. No one who lives in Him keeps on sinning. No one who continues to sin has either seen Him or known Him. 1 John 3: 1-6

You've heard the phrase, "You are your mother's child," People have said to me that I am looking more and more like my mother. That gives me great joy; I loved my mother so much. Of course, this also applies to our fathers, as well. If you look like your mother or father in a good way, that's admirable.

However, if someone has said that you look or act like either of your parents in a bad way that caused a negative seed to grow in you, denounce it right now; in Jesus Name. Because of the price that Jesus paid for us, we have been redeemed, washed in the blood, and made clean.

Beloved, if you are in Christ, no matter what anyone has said about you, or no matter what you have done, you are called, "children of God." That settles everything and silences all other voices of negativity, which causes inactivity, stunts your growth, and can lead to unfulfilled purpose. You have been made in the image and likeness of the Almighty God. Walk in it.

Let It Go

"Come to me, all you who are weary and burdened, and I will give you rest. Take my yoke upon you and learn from me, for I am gentle and humble in heart, and you will find rest for your souls. For my yoke is easy and my burden is light." Matthew 11: 28-30

In today's society it's difficult to focus with so many distractions begging for our attention. Driving by is the 'in thing.' Why, because, we've got to get to our next fifty appointments. We drive through our favorite fast food restaurant, we drive through the car wash, and we drive through to get our morning coffee.

Are we also driving through prayer? And, when we stop for that moment are we really giving our cares to the only One Who can solve them, or do we struggle to let them go? Worry causes stress, stress causes sickness, and sickness can cause…(we don't want to go there).

Beloved, Jesus' shoulders are much bigger than ours and capable of carrying anything that we give Him. What's also so great is that He already knows; He's just waiting on you to let it go.

It's Not How You Start, but How You Finish

"When they had gone, an angel of the Lord appeared to Joseph in a dream. "Get up," he said, "take the child and His mother and escape to Egypt. Stay there until I tell you, for Herod is going to search for the child to kill Him." Matthew 2: 13

The enemy tried to take Jesus out; he tried to kill Him at birth to stop the plan of God. "Herod gave orders to kill all the boys in Bethlehem and its vicinity who were two years old and under…" vs. 16.

Don't think that the enemy, Satan is passive, on the contrary, he has been trying to thwart God's plan since his fall from heaven (Isaiah 14: 12-17). He has been on assignment for you and me, as well, since we were born. God has a purpose for each of His children, and the enemy will use any circumstance to discourage, stop, and kill any plans the Lord may have for you.

You may have been born into a dysfunctional family, or may have been a product of divorced parents. Don't lose heart or give up, God's plan will prevail. Don't use excuses as to why you cannot fulfill the purpose for your life, instead seek God's direction and allow Him to finish what was started.

Is Your All On The Altar?

"After Jacob returned from Paddan Aram, God appeared to him again and blessed him. God said to him, "Your name is Jacob, but you will no longer be called Jacob; your name will be Israel." So He named him Israel. And God said to him, "I am God Almighty be fruitful and increase in number. A nation and a community of nations will come from you, and kings will come from your body. The land I gave to Abraham and Isaac I also give to you, and I will give this land to your descendants after you. Then God went up from him at the place where He had talked with him. Jacob set up a stone pillar at the place where God had talked with him, and he poured out a drink offering on it; he also poured oil on it. Jacob called the place where God had talked with him Bethel." Genesis 35: 9-15

God promised Jacob that through him nations would be birthed. It was there at the place where God spoke to Jacob that he built an altar; the place where he met God. Altars are places of worship and sacrifice; it was at the altar where Jacob received the promises of God. It was when Jacob met with God then after, that he built an altar.

Beloved, is your *all* on the altar? Our altars are places of sacrifice, and yes you can believe that the enemy will fight you to get there. But, go there! Have you forgotten the promises that God gave you? Go back to the altar and stay there.

Interception

"The righteous cry out, and the LORD hears them; He delivers them from all their troubles" Psalm 34: 17

Growing up with three older brothers I became accustomed to watching football on a regular basis, and have since grown to love the game. The best play of the game is, of course, the touchdown. However, another highlight in a football game is when the team that was down seven points and discouraged gets a ray of hope, receives an interception takes the ball from the opposing team, runs for 50 yards down the field and scores the touchdown. Jesus did that and more for us; we were on our way to hell and the enemy thought he had won. But, God had another plan.

He suffered and died, and was raised from the dead. He died for us and took the keys from the enemy. Now, we (believers) have eternal life. Not only did Christ die so that we could live, but He also came to give us the abundant life here on earth; He left us the Comforter, His Holy Spirit to be with us.

Beloved, if you're faced with pressures and things are overwhelming not knowing how you're going to make it, God will show up. He will intercept the plan of the enemy with His plan that will work out for your good. David said, *"I am still confident of this: I will see the goodness of the LORD in the land of the living. Wait for the Lord; be strong and take heart and wait for the LORD." Psalm 27: 13-14*

In Due Season

"Let us not become weary in doing good, for at the proper time we will reap a harvest if we do not give up." Galatians 6: 9

Any seed planted in the ground will one day grow and sprout up. I've never been one interested in gardening (though many say it is very relaxing)...those simple things in life, something to think about. Zondervan's commentary states that, "It's a natural law to reap what one sows."

If you sow love and kindness, you'll reap love and kindness. If you sow money, you'll reap money. If you sow discord, you'll reap dissension, envy, and division. What's interesting is that it only takes one seed to reap a multiple harvest; whether good or bad...something to think about. One apple seed will produce an apple tree. Wow!

Beloved, you've planted seeds of service, love, and possibly diligent study of the word of God. You've planted many seeds through giving of resources, and you may have planted and labored in the Lord's vineyard. Now, let time have its way. Though it may feel like your *waiting* has been in vain or is dormant. God is up to something (He always is), but soon and very soon your harvest will come.

I'm Going Fishing

"Afterward, Jesus appeared again to His disciples, by the Sea of Tiberias. It happened this way: Simon Peter, Thomas (called Didymus), Nathanael from Cana in Galilee, the sons of Zebedee, and two other disciples were together. "I'm going out to fish." Simon Peter told them, and they said, "We'll go with you." So they went out and got into the boat, but that night they caught nothing. Early in the morning, Jesus stood on the shore, but the disciples did not realize that it was Jesus. He called out to them, "Friends, haven't you any fish?" "No," they answered. He said, "Throw your net on the right side of the boat and you will find some." When they did, they were unable to haul the net in because of the large number of fish." John 21: 1-6

I used to be hard on the disciples thinking to myself, "Wow, after seeing the risen Savior, how could they go back to business as usual?" How could they go back to everyday hum drum? After being on this journey of growing in the Lord, I too have found myself in a momentary state of bewilderment. It's not unusual to wonder when the breakthrough will come, or when the promise will come. Don't beat yourself up if your faith has wavered. Don't be alarmed if you haven't seen results yet. Has it been that long? Isn't the Lord worth waiting for? Isn't He still on the throne?

Beloved, you may have tarried a long time and may have scars on your knees to show your diligence in prayer. But, I want to encourage you to hang in there and hold on to the Lord's promises. He is faithful. He will not let you down; never will He forsake you. Abraham waited twenty five years for the promise of a Son (Genesis 21: 5). Keep doing your part; continue to do what the Lord has said to do, keep waiting, and whatever you do, don't stop believing.

I'm Going Fishing (Plan B)

"Afterward, Jesus appeared again to His disciples, by the Sea of Tiberias. It happened this way: Simon Peter, Thomas (called Didymus), Nathanael from Cana in Galilee, the sons of Zebedee, and two other disciples were together. "I'm going out to fish." Simon Peter told them, and they said, "We'll go with you." So they went out and got into the boat, but that night they caught nothing. Early in the morning, Jesus stood on the shore, but the disciples did not realize that it was Jesus. He called out to them, "Friends, haven't you any fish?" "No," they answered. He said, "Throw your net on the right side of the boat and you will find some." When they did, they were unable to haul the net in because of the large number of fish." John 21: 1-6

The disciples spent a lot of time with Jesus before He was crucified and spent time with Him after His resurrection. During the time of His resurrection and ascension, they had decided to go back to what they were doing before. It is difficult to go back after you have been with the Savior. You've supped with Him; you've had powerful, intimate encounters with Him. How is it possible to go back? If you've given up everything for Him, is it easy to go back? Going back for some may mean, going back to a job. Maybe you left a job to step out on faith, believing that you heard the Lord say, "Go." But, you haven't seen the harvest yet. Or, perhaps, it is a mind-set that you're considering going back to. Do you have a plan B, in case this doesn't work out? Let me say this, there is no plan B with God, only plan A.

Beloved, you must remain steady to the task; remain steadfast in your believing, and in your doing what the Lord has said. He sees you and He sees your weariness. At a moment when the disciples were losing faith, Jesus shows up on the scene...I love that. Jesus is right there with you, as you go through. Don't stop on the way to your promise, to your deliverance, instead throw your net on the right side of the boat. In other words, try it again...keep going.

I'm Going Fishing (He's Not Done with You)

John 21: 1-6

I want to pose the question, haven't you been with Him, Jesus long enough to know Him, to trust Him, and to believe Him. If you're thinking of turning back...don't. Why? He is faithful, He is worthy. "God is not a man that He should lie, nor a son of man that He should change His mind..."(Numbers 23: 19). He will do what He said He will do. This is a word for you today...He is not done with you yet. Repeat after me, He is not done with me yet. Don't listen to the enemy's voice about anything. He lies that's all He does. "Jesus is the same yesterday, today, and forever" (Hebrews 13: 8). He changes not. He is not done with you. Paul tells us in Philippians 1: 6, "Being confident of this, that He Who began a good work in you will carry it on to completion until the day of Christ Jesus." He knows the plans He has for you, plans to prosper you, to do you know harm, and to give you a hope and a future (Jeremiah 29: 11).

Beloved, I encourage you to find two or three scriptures about what God has said to you and confess it, speak it, meditate on it. Get it down in your spirit that no devil in hell can take away from you, or stop you from believing what God has said to you. I believe it, because He said it; that's your resolve. You are not useless, dumb, or incompetent, you are not a drunk, you are not too old, to young, too black, too red, white, yellow, or whatever your uniqueness may be. You are the "called according to His purpose" (Romans 8: 28). He is not done with you yet.

I'm Going Fishing (Don't Turn Back)

"Afterward, Jesus appeared again to His disciples, by the Sea of Tiberias. It happened this way: Simon Peter, Thomas (called Didymus), Nathanael from Cana in Galilee, the sons of Zebedee, and two other disciples were together. "I'm going out to fish." Simon Peter told them, and they said, "We'll go with you." So they went out and got into the boat, but that night they caught nothing. Early in the morning, Jesus stood on the shore, but the disciples did not realize that it was Jesus. He called out to them, "Friends, haven't you any fish?" "No," they answered. He said, "Throw your net on the right side of the boat and you will find some." When they did, they were unable to haul the net in because of the large number of fish." John 21: 1-6

The disciples had witnessed the miracles and crucifixion; they had history with Him, but were lost. And, even after, could not produce one piece of fish to make a fish sandwich. Whew! Isn't that like us? We've been with the Master for a while. We have experienced His grace, mercy, His forgiveness. He has blessed us with all kinds of blessings and delivered us, but, now what's going on? Maybe you feel like you've thrown in your net and haven't caught a thing. You've fished all night...you've prayed, confessed, believed, but have not seen a thing. Don't turn back.

Beloved, do not turn back to the world; don't go back to the club, to the bottle, to brother-man, or sister-girl. Don't turn back to the things you once did, or once believed. Remember, in which you once believed. Paul tells the Galatians, "It is for freedom that Christ has set you free. Stand firm, and do not let yourselves be burdened. (Gal 5: 1). You were running a good race. Who cut in on you and kept you from obeying the truth? That kind of persuasion does not come from the One Who calls you (verse 7-8)." We need to stand firm and faithful. God hasn't forgotten you; in fact, He knows just where you are and just what you need. I encourage you to throw your net on the right side and don't turn back.

IF Now Is Not The Time, When?

"For the revelation awaits an appointed time; it speaks of the end and will not prove false. Though it linger, wait for it; it will certainly come and will not delay." Habakkuk 1: 13

Habakkuk had legitimate concerns that he brought before the Lord. He witnessed so much evil and perversion that it caused him to be distraught and it appeared as though evil was prevailing. So, he sought God for the answers. Have you ever wondered, "Where is God? Have you ever thought that God doesn't care, that maybe heaven has become like brass or that God doesn't hear your prayers? We cannot understand or explain everything that happens or understand God's timing. We must simply trust that God is sovereign, He is still on the throne, and that He will work things out for our good according to His purpose.

Beloved, there is an appointed time for everything. You may think now is the time for this or that, but God has set the appointed time for you. Just know that He is working. Don't lose heart and give up waiting or don't move ahead of God's appointed time.

"I Can Do It Myself"

"I am the Vine; you are the branches. If a man remains in Me and I in him, he will bear much fruit; apart from Me you can do nothing." John 15: 5

In the famous words of little 'Jake,' (name withheld to protect the innocent) "No, I can do it myself," instantly I heard deep within my spirit, the Lord telling me that is was me saying/doing the same thing. Immediately, I repented saying, "Father, forgive me when I tried to do things in my own strength...my own way.

I thank Him for quickening me to realize that the path that I had been on started with two sets of footprints, but only to fade to one set of footprints...my own. A few of us are doers. In fact, many of us can do many things at once (MT's...multi-taskers).

Beloved, go back to the place where you started...first base; the place where you sought the Lord night and day, and He gave you the *what* and the *when*. Allow Him to give you the *how*. Make sure you stay behind His footsteps and He will guide you all the way.

I Am the Resurrection

"Now a man named Lazarus was sick. He was from Bethany, the village of Mary and her sister Martha. This Mary, whose brother Lazarus now lay sick, was the same one who poured perfume on the Lord and wiped His feet with her hair. So the sisters sent word to Jesus, "Lord, the one you love is sick." When He heard this, Jesus said, "This sickness will not end in death. No, it is for God's glory so that God's Son may be glorified through it." Jesus loved Martha and her sister and Lazarus. Yet when He heard that Lazarus was sick, He stayed where He was two more days." John 11: 1-7

After the word of Lazarus' sickness was sent, the urgency of the sister's message, their anxiousness and need for Jesus to know that it was their brother who Jesus loved who was sick, Jesus stayed where He was two additional days. Wow! There is so much that we can learn.

First, Jesus is not in a hurry. He wasn't anxious and panicking, wondering, or puzzled about what He was going to do. He already knew what He planned to do (verse 4). Often times, we want to know why, this or that. Well, in this text, He tells us why, "It is for God's glory so that God's Son may be glorified through it." Why should the Resurrection, the giver of life, Elohim (Creator of all things), the One Who holds everything in His hands, the One Who created time need to be anxious? Your dead situation is only for "two days", or a season. Speak the very words that Jesus spoke, "This sickness will not end in death." Whatever your urgent matter is speak God's word over it, over and over and over.

Second, some of the people doubted Who Jesus was and so it is today. Beloved, you may believe, but those that are watching need to believe. Let Him be glorified in your situation, so that others may believe. We must let go so that He will be glorified, not us. Third, He cares. Jesus wept (verse 35). Jesus saw Mary weeping and said, "Where have you laid him?" He sees you weeping and is asking you, "Where have you laid your dead situation?" Give it to Him and watch Him resurrect it.

How to Hear From God

"I tell you the truth, the man who does not enter the sheep pen by the gate, but climbs in by some other way, is a thief and a robber. The man who enters by the gate is the shepherd of his sheep. The watchman opens the gate for him, and the sheep listen to His voice. He calls His own sheep by name and leads them out. When He has brought out all His own, He goes on ahead of them, and His sheep follow Him because they know His voice. But, they will never follow a stranger; in fact, they will run away from Him because they do not recognize a stranger's voice." John 10: 1-5

Beloved, have you ever had someone tell you something that caused you to question the validity of what was said? Did you investigate and critically seek to find the answer? In most cases, I would say yes. Why? Because, we should be open to not take statements at face value, without getting all of the facts; when in doubt an inquisitive mind would seek the truth. In this text, Jesus is telling us that He is the only way to the Father; He is the Gate.

I love how Jesus teaches with such simplicity that anyone can understand if their heart is open. To know the truth we must seek to know Jesus, and that can only be done through diligently studying His word. When we know His word, we know Him, and we will know His voice.

Just as sheep follow the shepherd and know his voice, so should any believer *know* the voice of Jesus. It takes time; it will not happen overnight. One must be committed. If you seek Him, you'll find Him (Matthew 7: 7). Begin to listen to His still small voice and soon you'll be able to discern between your own voice, the enemy's voice, and His voice.

Heaven on Earth

"Since, then, you have been raised with Christ, set your hearts on things above, where Christ is seated at the right hand of God. Set your minds on things above, not on earthly things. For you died, and your life is now hidden with Christ in God. When Christ, Who is your life, appears, then you also will appear with Him in glory." Colossians 3: 1-4

Colossians was written to combat heresy within the body of believers and to show that believers have everything they need in Christ. What does that say to you? It says that no matter what you or I are going through we have all that we need in Christ. We have all sufficiency in Him. You may be wondering, "What does that mean?" It means that the finished work of Christ settles it all. We do not need any material possession or anything else since Jesus has paid it all.

Having said that, we now can embrace contentment; realizing that God is in control and that we can have peace no matter what is going on. Jesus said, "Peace I leave with you; my peace I give you. I do not give to you as the world gives. Do not let your hearts be troubled and do not be afraid." John 14: 27

Beloved, yes, we will have troubles, but God has promised to be with us during our times of troubles. He has graciously given us the Holy Spirit, the Comforter, and our Sustainer Who will keep us. Let peace rule your life, instead of stress, worry, and anxiousness.

Heaven Bound

"Since, then you have been raised with Christ, set your hearts on things above, where Christ is seated at the right hand of God. Set your minds on things above, not on earthly things. For you died, and your life is now hidden with Christ in God. When Christ, Who is your life, appears, then you also will appear with Him in glory." Colossians 3: 1-4

In this text, Paul reminds the believers at the church of Colosse that their focus needs to be upward. In the first two chapters, he extinguishes all heresies that had made its way in the church. The word of God was given to us as a guide to help us in our Christian walk. It is still relevant today as it was when it was originally written. These stories that we read about are not fables; they are true events that happened and are available to us, to help us along the way. We don't have to struggle with our issues; we can look at the manual for direction. The word of God is like a transparency, in that, it is a clear tool used for the purpose of holding things together, while at the same time, has the ability to see through it. In the same way, the bible allows us to see ourselves, at the same time, it holds us together.

Beloved, just as Paul exhorts, we must, "set our hearts on things above..." In essence, do the things pleasing to God, or be about His business. Yes, we live in a corrupt fallen world that is perishing daily. However, we know that earth is not our home; we're just passing through. Don't get too wrapped up in the affairs of this world, rather be heavenly focused and purpose driven.

Having a Right Heart

"Hear the word of the LORD, you rulers of Sodom; listen to the law of our God, you people of Gomorrah! "The multitude of your sacrifices, what are they to me?" says the LORD. "I have more than enough of burnt offerings, of rams and the fat of fattened animals; I have no pleasure in the blood of bulls and lambs and goats. When you come to appear before me, who has asked this of you, this trampling of my courts? Stop bringing me meaningless offerings! Your incense is detestable to me, New Moons, Sabbaths and convocations. I cannot bear your evil assemblies. Your New Moon festivals and your appointed feasts my soul hates. They have become a burden to me; I am weary of bearing them." Isaiah 1: 10-14

The sacrifices were detestable to God, because they were not done with a sincere heart. They were faithful with the 'system of offerings and sacrifices', but were far from His heart. Beloved, at some point we all must do a self-inventory of our hearts, and clean out those areas that have become stale or have fallen prey to sin...a circumcision of the heart. Why? I'm glad you asked.

It's easy to just go through the motions of day to day tasks...off to work we go, come home, sit in front of the television, wake up the next day, and do the same thing all over again. We can become so predictable in our doing that we may be able to do these things in our sleep. Pause for a moment and let that resonate.

Do we have the same attitude about God? Do we week after week go to church, come home, and then do it all over again with no change or true devotion and worship for the King? It's a simple solution...turn.

Go Deep

"When He had finished speaking, He said to Simon, "Put out into deep water, and let down the nets for a catch." Luke 5: 4

Peter was a fisherman by trade, a master fisherman at best, I can only imagine. Since this was his 'bread and butter,' he was frustrated and must have wondered when his provision would come through (read the full account). At times, we too may rely on our own abilities rather than the sovereignty of God.

Did you know that Jesus is concerned about everything that concerns you, yes, even those deep things? I'll say it again; Jesus is concerned about **everything** that concerns you. No one else can carry or has carried our burdens like Jesus. He hears you and He cares.

Beloved, Jesus died to set us free from death's trap, but to also set us free from the enemy's taunts and accusations of worry and doubt. I know that you may be saying, "I've been praying and nothing is happening." Like Peter saying, "Master, we've worked hard all night and haven't caught anything, (vs.5)" you may need to go deeper...fast, pray, and keep praying. Worry about nothing, pray about everything.

Giving Thanks

Give thanks to the LORD, for He is good, His love endures forever. Give thanks to the God of gods, His love endures forever. Give thanks to the Lord of lords, His love endures forever. To Him Who alone does great wonders, His love endures forever. Psalm 136: 1-4

Beloved, let this day be a day of reflection of the goodness of our Lord and Savior, Jesus Christ. Reflect on His grace and His mercy that endures forever. Give thanks for the essentials, give thanks for the non-essentials. Give thanks that your name is written in the book of life...give thanks. Give thanks that He is with you and that He will never leave you, nor forsake you...give thanks.

Reflect on today and days passed that He has brought you through and will continue to. We can live without many things, but be most thankful that we cannot live without Him and that He has made it possible (if you are His child) that we never have to.

If you have never accepted Jesus as your Lord and Savior, I extend an invitation for you to come. "...confess with your mouth, "Jesus is Lord," and believe in your heart that God raised Him from the dead, you will be saved. For it is with your heart that you believe and are justified, and it is with your mouth that you confess and are saved." (Romans 10: 9-10)

"For God so loved the world that He have His one and only Son, that whoever believes in Him shall not perish but have eternal life." John 3: 16

Give Thanks

"Be joyful always; pray continually; give thanks in all circumstances, for this is God's will for you in Christ Jesus." 1 Thessalonians 5: 16-18

I am most thankful for the Lord Jesus Christ, because of Who He is. I am thankful, because no matter what life may throw at me it doesn't matter because Jesus is with me, and that He will work out everything for my good. I am thankful for my family, good health, and that I have basic necessities; I can't complain about anything.

My heart weeps for those who are less fortunate, for those who don't have basic necessities, and unfortunately in the richest nation in the world, America many are without. Just the other day as I was walking into a store, a man stopped me and asked me for .35 cents. I heard the Lord say, *"Give."* I'm thankful that I had more than .35 cents to give him.

Beloved, what are you thankful for today? Be content in what you have, but mostly be thankful for Jesus Christ. *"Thanks be to God for His indescribable gift" 2 Corinthians 9: 15*

Give God Your Best

Leviticus 1: 10-13

"If the offering is a burnt offering from the flock, from either the sheep or the goats, he is to offer a male without defect. He is to slaughter it at the north side of the altar before the Lord, and Aaron's sons the altar on all sides. He is to cut it into pieces, and the priest shall arrange them, including the head and the fat, on the burning wood that is on the altar. He is to wash the inner parts and the legs with water, and the priest is to bring all of it and burn it on the altar. It is a burnt offering, an offering made by fire, an aroma pleasing to the Lord."

The offering that the priest would sacrifice was to be spotless; there were specific instructions that God gave them to do as atonement for the sins of the people. These instructions from God were very detailed and clear and they were given to show sinful people how they could relate to a Holy God, and not to take their relationship with Him lightly. We too are to reverence God and to walk in holiness for He is Holy, and as His children we are to be holy like Him.

"An aroma pleasing to the Lord," means that God accepted the people's attitude. How is your attitude toward God and serving Him? Do we serve out of obligation or under duress? Do we complain? Our service to Him should be just as the animal that was sacrificed, spotless, excellent, and given with a pure heart.

With our time, talent, and treasure we give to God. (1) Our time should be served with diligence, timeliness (arriving on time to serve, in fact be early), and even at times sacrifice (2) Our talent should be given to God, in fact, He is the one that gave it to us, give your talent better than you gave it to the world (3) Our treasure...just let it go, God can't bless us abundantly until we let it go. Let Him multiply it.

GET ME OUT OF HERE!

"But the LORD provided a great fish to swallow Jonah, and Jonah was inside the fish three days and three nights. From inside the fish Jonah prayed to the LORD his God. He said: "In my distress I called to the LORD, and he answered me. From the depths of the grave I called for help, and you listened to my cry." Jonah 1: 17, 2: 1-2

The purpose of this account is to show the *all-inclusive* grace of God and His love for all people and His desire that "no one perish," (2 Peter 3: 9). If I may draw your attention to the urgency of Jonah's plight, his repentance and ultimate surrender should allow us to empathize with his state. Jonah, as we know, ran from the Lord and wound up in a deep situation that only God could get him out of. Wow! Have you been swallowed up by something much larger than you? Three days and three nights tell me that there is an end. Remember that. There is an end. Jesus quoted this story (Matthew 12: 40) telling of his purpose and victory.

Beloved, I believe that the Lord is telling us to draw nigh to Him. Our friends can be comforting to us in times of crisis, but they don't have the answer only God has the answer. Surrender to whatever He may be telling you and know this that when you cry out to Him...He will answer.

Get In By Yourself

"At that time, the Kingdom of Heaven will be like ten virgins who took their lamps and went out to meet the bridegroom. Five of them were foolish and five were wise. The foolish ones took their lamps but did not take any oil with them. The wise, however, took oil in jars along with their lamps. The bridegroom was a long time in coming, and they all became drowsy and fell asleep. At midnight the cry rang out, 'Here's the bridegroom! Come out to meet Him! "Then all the virgins woke up and trimmed their lamps. The foolish ones said to the wise, 'Give us some of your oil; our lamps are going out.' "No," they replied, 'there may not be enough for both of us and you. Instead, go to those who sell oil and buy some for yourselves.' But while they were on their way to buy oil, the bridegroom arrived. The virgins who were ready went in with Him to the wedding banquet. And the door was shut." Matthew 25: 1-10

It's foolish for one to think that they can get into heaven on the testimony or faith of someone else…father, mother, grandmother, or a friend. It's also foolish for one to think that it is possible to ride on someone else's anointing. The cost is too high…it's personal.

No one can read the bible for you, no one can study for you, no one can serve for you, and no one can believe for you. This type of mindset or attitude Jesus refers to as a lazy servant (25: 26). It is a sacrifice of time, talent, and resources.

Beloved, spiritual preparation can't be bought or borrowed at any time (LASB). Will you be ready? Will you be ready to meet the Savior? Tomorrow is not promised. Ask Jesus to come into your heart. "That if you confess with your mouth, "Jesus is Lord," and believe in your heart that God raised Him from the dead, you will be saved." Romans 10: 9

From Opulence to Obscurity

"After forty years had passed, an angel appeared to Moses in the flames of a burning bush in the desert near Mount Sinai."
Acts 7: 30

According to the bible, Moses was the humblest man on the earth (Numbers 12: 3). In Stephen's account (Acts 7) he exhorts in his speech to the Sanhedrin counsel, "...he was no ordinary child." God had a plan for his life; He was ordering the steps of Moses the whole time. From shepherd to deliverer, his feet did not always tread upon gold streets dressed in purple linen. On the contrary, though highly esteemed later in life, he was divinely spared from the hand of Pharoah (Exodus 1:22) at birth. Yes, he grew up in the palace and was reared in the finest educational institutions of that time. However, that was not his destiny. God had another plan. And, though he like us messed up...missed the mark, his God-given purpose was fulfilled. Moses spent forty years tending sheep before hearing one word from God...something to think about.

Beloved, it may seem like you've been living on the back hills of Midian in a desert place, a solitary place. But, be of good cheer God knows where you are. He knows your address, phone number, email, and He does not need to like you on Facebook. He knows exactly what you need. He knows what it takes and how long It must take to prepare you for what He has for you. It may not be a place of glamour or overflow; rather, it will be a place where He has specifically and purposefully designed for you. Does it matter how long? Hmm, it took ***forty short years*** for Moses.

Freedom vs Discipline

"Though I am free and belong to no man, I make myself a slave to everyone, to win as many as possible. To the Jews I became like a Jew, to win the Jews. To those under the law I became like one under the law (though I myself am not under the law), so as to win those under the law. To those not having the law I became like one not having the law (though I am not free from God's law but am under Christ's law), so as to win those not having the law. To the weak I became weak, to win the weak. I have become all things to all men so that by all possible means I might save some. I do all this for the sake of the gospel that I may share in its blessings." 1 Corinthians 9: 19-23

I am so inspired by the Apostle Paul; he sought the Lord and ran his race with such determination. In this text, he is telling the believers at Corinth his "how to plan," or strategic plan in "becoming all things to win some..." Yet, though Paul is free in Christ, free from bondages, strongholds, material drive, or positions, he did not use his freedom to sin, to flaunt, or to be puffed up. He disciplined himself for the goal of winning many to Christ. He did not get side-tracked or distracted.

Beloved, our ultimate goal in whatever we do, or are purposed to do should be to glorify God in our lives. We only have one earthly life to live and a short one, compared to eternity. If you don't know your purpose ask God, the One who created you. Don't waste time or use your freedom in things that the Lord has not ordained, rather seek and do those things that He has uniquely designed for you. Get on His plan, His road; then will you find peace. And, if you are not sure continue doing what you are doing, until He re-directs you.

Follow the Leader

"Since we live by the Spirit, let us keep in step with the Spirit."
Galatians 5: 25

A few years back we lived near a pond, and often I would see the geese fly in and out of the pond. I'd watch the mother goose take off on ground and the baby geese would follow right behind her. It was so amazing to watch...wherever she stepped they stepped. It looked like a military squad formation in perfect cadence like soldiers following their leader.

When our children were small, at times when we were out shopping or running errands, they would have a tendency to run ahead of us. I would tell them to watch how the baby geese follow the mother goose and to emulate them.

Beloved, if we're not careful we too will run ahead of God or the leading of the Holy Spirit. We must keep in step with Him, if not; we'll experience unnecessary anxiousness, struggle, and trouble. It's very simple; just keep in step with Him.

Faith

"So we see that they were not able to enter, because of their unbelief." Hebrews 3: 19

Some of the Israelites did not enter the rest of God, because of unbelief; they doubted even after He delivered them from Pharaoh, fed them manna, and provided shelter for them day and night. Most of the first generation did not enter the Promised Land (Numbers 14: 20-23). They had spiritual amnesia, forgetting what the Lord had done, as well as, they began worshiping idols, grumbling, and complaining. Sound familiar? We too can fall prey to the deceitfulness, distractions, and the traps of the enemy by not believing, or forgetting what God has already done. Though the wait may seem long, God has not forgotten you. Just look back and remember what the Lord has done in the past, and believe and trust that He will do the same right now.

The lack of faith in God is believing the lie that God is not able and we know where that school of thought came from...the devil. You see, sometimes we have selective faith; the kind of faith that believes that He could do that, but surely He couldn't do this. Sometimes, trials come to test our faith, no matter where you are in your walk with God. Trust Him, and go through the journey. Finish the race.

Beloved, are you struggling in your faith? If so, read all of the stories of the patriarchs in the bible. Read about their trials and tests; you'll discover that they too had a journey and many battles to overcome. You will be blessed and encouraged. *"Is anything too hard for the Lord?"* Genesis 18: 14

Faith First

"Therefore, the promise comes by faith, so that it may be by grace and may be guaranteed to all Abraham's offspring, not only to those who are of the law but also to those who are of the faith of Abraham. He is the father of us all." Romans 4: 16

Abraham believed God before the manifestation of the promise. He simply had the childlike faith believing that what God said He would do...He would do. What is childlike faith? It is the kind of faith that is unmovable. When you were young did your father or mother promise to do something, or to take you somewhere and you waited all day long, telling your friends about what you were expecting, and no matter how long it took them to get there, you still waited and believed? That's the kind of faith that you have to have.

Sometimes, you may ask why it takes so long. I can't answer that question for you, because every situation and circumstance is different, and God may be doing something different in your life than in someone else's life. Maybe, the Lord is building your faith, or simply getting you ready or preparing you for what you are waiting for. Never take His delay as denial, unless He has said no, rather, keep the faith, walk a pure and a holy life, do what you can do to be ready. Keep pursuing God, not His hand, but Him. *"And without faith it is impossible to please God, because anyone who comes to Him must believe that He exists and that He rewards those who earnestly seek Him." Hebrews 11: 6*

Empty Your Vessel, Fill It With God

"When an evil spirit comes out of a man, it goes through arid places seeking rest and does not find it. Then it says, I will return to the house I left. When it arrives, it finds the house unoccupied, swept clean and put in order. Then it goes and takes with it seven other spirits more wicked than itself, and they go in and live there. And the final condition of that man is worse than the first." Matthew 12: 43-45

In this chapter we read how the Pharisees (teachers of the Law) were trying to "trip up" Jesus, asking for a sign. They knew the law; they knew what was foretold by the prophets, but they still would not recognize Jesus as the Messiah. Why, because, Jesus' mission did not line up with their theology. He did not come as a conquering king to overrule Roman oppression; rather He came to save those who were lost and to establish His spiritual kingdom; all for the sake of love. Jesus knew the hearts of the Pharisees; they were clean on the outside adorned in their robes with long tassels, praying in public, and fasting to be seen by men. But, they were full of evil on the inside.

Beloved, we can clean up the outer and neglect the inner. It is possible to clean up our lives, emptying those things that are not of God by not doing things that we used to do, or by not going to places that we used to go. But, what is critical is that we must fill our vessels with the word of God, prayer, praise and worship, and a renewed infilling of the Holy Spirit daily. If not, our empty vessels can be filled with other things that are not of God, which will open up the door for the enemy. Keeping our vessels full of God takes effort, it will not come automatically. To be spiritually strong we must exercise spiritual devotions regularly.

Eat For Strength

"The angel of the Lord came back a second time and touched him and said, "Get up and eat, for the journey is too much for you." So he got up and ate and drank. Strengthened by that food, he traveled forty days and forty nights until he reached Horeb, the mountain of God." 1 Kings 19: 7-8

After the Lord gave Elijah victory in killing the 850 prophets of Baal, he began to feel distressed as Jezebel sought after his life so he ran and hid. Often, after a great victory you may experience a low period, condemnation, or guilt. Just know that those feelings or thoughts are from the enemy; they are not from the Lord. Like Elijah, you may have been blessed with something that you have been praying for or gotten victory in an area, but then find yourself feeling overwhelmed or that you should have done this or that.

Beloved, don't hide or withdraw and start believing those thoughts, and definitely do not begin to speak them into existence. Instead draw strength from the Lord and begin meditating and feeding on the word of God to find strength. Just as the Lord told Elijah, your journey is too much for you. Get up and eat and drink. Eat on the word of God and drink the refreshing water of the Holy Spirit. The enemy will try to oppress you, but fight him with the word of God and in the power of the Holy Spirit. You have an assignment and in order to do it, you need rest and strength in the Lord.

"Jesus answered, "It is written: 'Man does not live on bread alone, but on every word that comes from the mouth of God." Matthew 4: 4

Double Portion

"There was a certain man from Ramathaim, a Zuphite from the hill country of Ephraim, whose name was Elkanah son of Jeroham, the son of Elihu, the son of Tohu, the son of Zuph, an Ephraimite. He had two wives; one was called Hannah and the other Peninnah. Peninnah had children, but Hannah had none. Year after year this man went up from his town to worship and sacrifice to the Lord Almighty at Shiloh, where Hophni and Phinehas, the two sons of Eli, were priests of the Lord. Whenever the day came for Elkanah to sacrifice, he would give portions of the meat to his wife Peninnah and to all her sons and daughters. But to Hannah he gave a double portion because the Lord had closed her womb." 1 Samuel 1: 1-5

Have you ever noticed how when you're going through something that it seems as though your focus is primarily on your problem or situation? You may find yourself thinking about it when you rise in the morning, at mid-day, evening, and it's on your mind when you go to sleep. The enemy tries to keep you focused on your problem and everything negative instead on focusing on everything positive in your life; what God has already done.

In verse 5, the scripture says, "Hannah received a double portion, because the Lord had closed her womb. She was blessed although her womb was closed. Stop looking at what's wrong in your life and look at what's good and praise God.

You may be experiencing challenges or trials in one area, but look at the other areas that are blessed. You may be in need of a job, but you and your family are healthy; you have been given a double portion. God hears your prayers and He will answer in His time, relax. In Isaiah 61:7, it states "Instead of their shame, my people will receive a double portion...". Trust Him. Rejoice and be glad for what the Lord is doing in your life now as you continue to patiently wait for what He is going to do.

Don't Stop Building

"Then I prayed to the God of heaven, and I answered the king,
"If it pleases the king and if your servant has found favor in his
sight, let him send me to the city in Judah where my fathers are
buried so that I can rebuild it." Nehemiah 2: 5

The wall represented protection; with no wall the Jews were
vulnerable to the attacks of their enemies. After the exile, being
free from bondage they became complacent, and in turn, began
to make excuses for not finishing the work that had been
started. In 2008, came a whirlwind of downsizing, high
unemployment rates, and foreclosures. And, many became
discouraged by allowing a temporary setback stop them from
persevering. However, God can bring an uprising . Are you
ready to begin rebuilding again? It's time to build; it's time to
finish the project, refocus and get back in the race.

Beloved, anything worth building can be a daunting task, but is
well worth the effort. Don't let a season of setbacks stop what
you started to build. There will be distractions, delays, and
discouragement, but don't stop.

Don't Turn Away

"Dear friends, although I was eager to write to you about the salvation we share, I felt I had to write and urge you to contend for the faith that was once for all entrusted to the saints...But, dear friends, remember what the apostles of our Lord Jesus Christ foretold. They said to you, "In the last times there will be scoffers who will follow their own ungodly desires. These men who divide you, who follow mere natural instincts and do not have the Spirit, but you dear friends, build yourselves up in your most holy faith and pray in the Holy Spirit. Keep yourselves in God's love as you wait for the mercy of our Lord Jesus Christ to bring you to eternal life." Jude 1: 3, 17-21

It's easy to get caught up in the fast pace of this world. It takes a commitment, a loyal sold out heart, and a tenacious spirit to stand. You will stand out...a peculiar people, don't be alarmed. They will talk about you, but remember they talked about and persecuted our Lord. The enemy will show you all the kingdoms of this world (Matthew 4:4), but will you bow down? Don't fall for the enticements. You are a remnant, one who remains true to Christ and refuses to leave.

Beloved, we are living in the last days and are experiencing the beginning of birth pains (Matthew 24: 4-8), in which Jesus spoke of. Don't turn away from Him, don't believe or follow the standards of this world, rather, turn to Him. Father, help us to not become consumed with the things of this world...to not compromise, but to always be transformed by the renewing of our minds.

Don't Leave Home without Him

*"After His suffering, He showed Himself to these men and gave many convincing proofs that He was alive. He appeared to them over a period of forty days and spoke about the Kingdom of God. On one occasion, while he was eating with them, He gave them this command: "Do not leave Jerusalem, but **wait** for the gift my Father promised, which you have heard me speak about. For John baptized with water, but in a few days you will be baptized with the Holy Spirit." Acts 1: 3-5*

The book of Acts chronicles the birth of the church, and it details Paul's missionary journeys. In the beginning of the book, Jesus is giving the disciples His final instructions. He tells them not to leave for Jerusalem, but to wait for the gift that was promised by the Father. Key word is **wait.**

When a person receives Jesus Christ as Lord and Savior, The Holy Spirit dwells in them. Jesus is no longer physically here on earth, but He lives inside every believer. The Holy Spirit is the *dunamis* (Greek word, which means dynamite) power that enabled the disciples to spread the gospel. This same power is within us and it enables and empowers us to do what God has created us to do, and to become a new creation in Christ Jesus. The Holy Spirit is our Comforter, Counselor, and our Guide; He gives us direction.

When facing decisions, do you ask the Holy Spirit, Who knows all things? Or, do you make a decision without Him? We usually make sure that before we leave home we have our ID, cash, debit card, insurance cards, and of course our cell phones (How would we ever survive without them) etc. before leaving the house. How much more important is it to seek the counsel of the Holy Spirit before making a decision. Ask, seek, and wait.

Do It Any Way

"Now Jericho was tightly shut up because of the Israelites, no one went out and no one came in. Then, the Lord said to Joshua, "See, I have delivered Jericho into your hands, along with its king and its fighting me. March around the city once with all the armed men. Do this for six days. Have seven priests carry trumpets of rams; horns in from of the ark. On the seventh day, march around the city seven times, with the priests blowing the trumpets. When you hear them sound a long blast on the trumpets, have all the people give a loud shout; then the wall of the city will collapse and the people will go up, every man straight in." Joshua 6: 1-5

We set out to do a task and often times find ourselves running in several directions, and out of breath. We may think about it, investigate it, organize it, and then we move. Then, what happens? We crash and suddenly we realize that we forgot something, or should I say someone…the Lord. OMG, we forgot to ask Him. We did not get His direction; we did not listen for His voice. Why, we've become independent and self-sufficient, and too hurried. God knows the plan He has for us (Jeremiah 29: 11) and His plan is perfect. We may not understand what or why He is telling us to do certain things, but that doesn't matter, **do it anyway**. The Lord gave Joshua and Israel specific instructions; the victory was already theirs, but obedience to every detail was critical.

Beloved, we must do what the Lord says, it's not an option. If you've taken steps without Him, don't fret we've all done it. Stop, look up, and ask Him to forgive you for moving without Him and to re-direct you. Stay in your lane, stay true to your assignment. Yes we do need to plan, prepare, and move, but we don't have to worry or be anxious about how we will accomplish what He has said; all we have to do is **do it anyway**. And, remember to do exactly what He says (don't deviate) and to continually seek Him. He will be there to help, guide, and provide.

Distractions

"Why, you do not even know what will happen tomorrow. What is your life? You are a mist that appears for a little while and then vanishes." James 4: 14

We are bombarded with so many things that capture our attention. It's no wonder that at times we lose our focus. If you asked yourself the question, "How many times a day am I distracted by something, the phone, the internet, television, matters on the job, or relationships? What would be your answer? Some of these distractions can pull you in such a direction that you are not productive; productive, not busy, and there is a difference. However, at the end of the day, all of our doing can absolutely mean nothing if we are not doing it to help others or for the sake of Christ.

Beloved, we only have a few years here on earth compared to forever in eternity with Christ. Whatever you're purposed to do now is the time to do it; not tomorrow, but today. The old adage that says, "Don't put off tomorrow what you can do today," is still relevant. God may be calling you to do something...do it, or maybe you're someone who has not accepted Jesus as your Lord and Savior. Don't put it off any longer...do it.

Do What He Says

"Do not merely listen to the word, and so deceive yourselves. Do what it says. Anyone who listens to the word but does not do what it says is like a man who looks at his face in a mirror and, after looking at himself, goes away and immediately forgets what he looks like. But the man who looks intently into the perfect law that gives freedom, and continues to do this, not forgetting what he has heard, but doing it; he will be blessed in what he does." James 1: 22-25

Our physical face is only a reflection, an outer covering or a mask of who we really are. We are made of spirit, soul, and body. First, God breathed the breath of life into us and we became a living soul, then He clothed us in a body, just as He created man in the beginning. God told Jeremiah, "Before I formed you in the womb I knew you."

God knew us the same way as He did Jeremiah before we were born. If we want to know what we really look like, look in the word, not in the mirror. Don't focus on the outer; rather, focus on the inner by developing the character of Christ in you, which can only happen by renewing your mind (Romans 12: 2).

Beloved, we renew our mind (soul-heart, thoughts, feelings, and attitudes) through the word of God. We have been taught or conditioned by the world (society), our environment, traditions, and even our own families. Our own intellectual reasoning and ideologies mean nothing as a Christian. To be born again, born of the Spirit means a new life, a changed life; a new way of living doing it by the word of God. If we say we are a Christian then we follow the example of Christ.

Can You or Can You Not?

"Flee the evil desires of youth, and pursue righteousness, faith, love and peace, along with those who call on the Lord out of a pure heart." 2 Timothy 2: 22

Last week, I went three days without continual use of my cell phone, because my battery was going out. I didn't have it to look at every 30 seconds; you know what I mean. We've become so used to these little technological devices that it is almost debilitating. Speaking for myself, I felt anxious and panicked that I had missed an important call or text. I thought, "Oh no, what if someone is trying to call me." At that moment, I could hear the Holy Spirit say, "What did you do before cell phones?" Immediately, I realized that I had gone to a far place, a place of dependency and desperation, resulting in pre-occupation. I had allowed myself to almost self-destruct over a small hand held device.

Beloved, Paul exhorts Timothy as his young mentee, and all Christians to, "flee the evil desires of youth..." I am not suggesting that having a cell phone is evil, rather, if it becomes a god (small 'g'), in that, we spend more time with it than God, The Father, it is evil and has become an idol. Let's not become so dependent on these conveniences and allow them to draw our time away from the Lord. Perhaps, for you it's not your cell phone, but It's a person, or some other sin.

We must flee (run like you have stolen something; I'm kidding, just an old phrase) those things that we exalt and give our most attention to. Can you live without it? Well, in order to keep up our fast pace, I would say no. However, take time out to see how much time you spend with your phone, than with the Lord. Are you out of balance?

Boot Camp

"Do you not know that in a race all the runners run, but only one gets the prize? Run in such a way as to get the prize. Everyone who competes in the games goes into strict training. They do it to get a crown that will not last; but we do it to get a crown that will last forever. Therefore, I do not run like a man running aimlessly; I do not fight like a man beating the air. No, I beat my body and make it my slave so that after I have preached to others, I myself will not be disqualified for the prize." 1 Corinthians 9: 24-27

Paul, after being converted on the road to Damascus, devoted his life for Christ. Paul began his ministry around the age of 60; he didn't use the excuse, "I'm too old, or it's too late." No, instead he ran his race with vigor, stamina, and with urgency. Paul was disciplined and determined, and he exhorts the Corinthian believers, as well as, all believers to live with the same determination.

Joseph, at the age of seventeen had a dream and told his brothers. He had to endure years of 'training' of preparation. He was thrown in a pit, sold into slavery, and was falsely accused and spent time in prison. Though, a tough journey, Joseph's journey was that of intensity and pressure, but it equipped him for his assignment (Genesis 37, 39-50).

Beloved, don't take discipline or tough times for granted. Why? There is purpose in your pain. You may not see it now, but your spiritual muscles are becoming stronger and stronger. Your ability to endure is reaching maturity. Hold on. Don't quit in the middle of your "personal training" session. Everyone's journey is different, and is uniquely designed to fit God's purpose. And, it is only for a season.

Believe Until You See It

"Now the Lord was gracious to Sarah as He had said, and the Lord did for Sarah what He had promised. Sarah became pregnant and bore a son to Abraham in his old age, at the very time God had promised Him. Abraham gave the name Isaac to the son Sarah bore him. Abraham was a hundred years old when his son Isaac was born to him." Genesis 21: 1-3, 5

At the age of seventy-five God told Abraham, "Leave your country, your people and your father's household and go to the land I will show you. I will make you into a great nation and I will bless you (Genesis 12: 1-2)." Twenty five years later, at the age of one hundred Isaac was born. Though it was twenty five years before the promised was fulfilled, God did what He said He would do. Abraham had to wait on God, and no matter what happened or no matter what Abraham did (He did make some mistakes along the way), God's promise manifested at the appointed time. I'm not advocating blatant sin and disobedience; I'm simply saying that if you've messed up, repent, get back on track, obey God, and continue to wait.

Beloved, there is an appointed time of your promise. Just because you don't see it now, doesn't mean that it will not happen. Don't be bothered by what you see, wait on God like Abraham. Go get yourself a bulldog faith that says, "I don't care what it looks like I believe God." Build your faith muscles by continuing in His word and confessing the word over your promise, and stay joyful. Don't worry about how long it is taking; a watched clock never seems to move. Keep serving, and don't stop believing it shall come to pass.

Being Thankful

"Be joyful always; pray continually; give thanks in all circumstances, for this is God's will for you in Christ Jesus." 1 Thessalonians 5: 16-18

Paul's charge to the believers at Thessalonica in this verse is to strengthen them. It is to remind them to be thankful at all times, and that their joy and thanksgiving should not falter depending on circumstances, rather it should remain at all times.

Being thankful for even the little things goes a long way. Do you have a roof over your head, a thermostat in which you can regulate the heat? Do you have food (not steak or lobster), clothing (at least one outfit), and at least one pair of shoes? Do you have a loved one or a friend; one whom you can call? If you answered yes to any of these questions, then you are blessed and can be very thankful. If we all made a list of everything that we have, I'm sure that we would have more to be thankful for than not.

Beloved, most of all, being thankful that we are sons and daughters of the Most High and that we have *"All sufficiency in Him"* brings things into the right perspective.

Armed and Dangerous (Part 1)

"Finally, be strong in the Lord and in His mighty power. Put on the full armor of God so that you can take your stand against the devil's schemes. For our struggle is not against flesh and blood, but against the rulers, against the authorities, against the powers of this dark world and against the spiritual forces of evil in the heavenly realms. Therefore put on the full armor of God, so that when the day of evil comes, you may be able to stand your ground, and after you have done everything, to stand."
Ephesians 6: 10-13

Do you know that you have an enemy? Do you know that through Christ as His child He has empowered you with spiritual weapons to fight against the enemy's schemes? But, often we forget that we are loaded with spiritual weapons and by the time we come to the realization, the enemy has temporarily defeated us. I say, temporarily, because we have already won the battle through Christ at the cross, and through the resurrection. He is subtle; he will not appear in dragon attire, but will appear attractive, good, and very smooth. He himself will not appear, but will use others to do his dirty work. He's not trying to hurt your feelings; rather, he is trying to destroy you. The enemy, who is not seen, is very real. Therefore, we cannot fight in the flesh we must fight in the spirit.

Our first weapon, the belt of truth encompasses everything that Jesus is. In Christ, we carry His belt of truth, because His Spirit lives within us, the Spirit of Truth (John 14: 17). Our second weapon, the breastplate of righteousness is there to guard our heart, our most inward emotion. Without righteousness we leave ourselves open to the attacks and temptations of the enemy. God's righteousness replaces our filthy clothes of sin with what Jesus did for us. Are you ready for battle? It's war...

Armed and Dangerous (Part 2)

Ephesians 6: 10-13

Paul tells the believers in Ephesus and believers everywhere that the "day of evil" will come. As long as we are in this earthly suit, we will encounter opposition and attacks from the enemy. He is letting us know to expect it. But, we can relax and not worry, because we have been given mighty, powerful, spiritual weapons to stand. Our third weapon is 'feet fitted with the Gospel of peace.' One the tricks of the enemy is to distract us, if he can get us to focus on our problem, then most likely we're too preoccupied to tell others the good news of Jesus. It is the good news of the gospel that sets people free. Jesus said, "So, if the Son sets you free you will be free indeed." (John 8: 36) Sometimes we think that it's too hard to tell others about Christ, so we don't say anything.

We need to be ready at all times to share the gospel. When we allow the enemy to attack our mind or pollute it with so much junk, in turn, we focus on those things to the point of pre-occupation that we neglect to tell others about Christ. The attacks come in the form of: fear, doubt, and insecurity, so why bother, right? However, with our feet fitted, grounded, or secure in Christ and His power and knowing He is with us gives us the power and peace to do what He has told us to do. The fourth weapon, shield of faith surrounds us. Our faith can stand against anything...unbelief, lack, or tormenting spirits of shame and condemnation. Our faith is tangible and proven (Ephesians 2: 8) (Hebrews 11: 1), and it will deflect every fiery dart from the enemy. Stay anointed.

Armed and Dangerous (Part 3)

Ephesians 6: 10-13

In this fallen world in which we live lies beneath the surface of all evil, Satan. He is cunning and deceptive. His agenda is to totally take out believers in Christ. Jesus said, "The thief comes *only* to steal, kill, and to destroy; but I have come that they may have life, and have it to the full (John 10: 10). Take note of the 'only;' his goal is only to destroy us. We do not have to fear, because we have been given mighty weapons to combat the enemy's attack. Our spiritual weapons are more powerful than any physical weapon.

The fifth weapon is the helmet of salvation. The helmet is made to protect the head; it is worn at all times during combat. The brain sets things in motion; the control panel. The enemy will attack your mind with thoughts of failure, insecurity, and unbelief, which can cause negative actions. Colossians 3: 2 states that we are to, "Set our mind on things above, not on earthly things." 1 Corinthians 1: 16, "...But we have the mind of Christ." As a soldier trains for battle, we too must train our minds; we are to renew our minds (Romans 12: 2). The more we feed our minds with the knowledge of Jesus, we are defeating the enemy.

Our sixth weapon, the sword of the Spirit, is the word of God. This is the only offensive weapon of all; we are to fight the enemy by using God's word, believing and speaking it out. We must be vigilant, alert at all times. A soldier in the armed forces is trained to be watchful at all times; he/she is disciplined. Soldiers regularly clean and inspect their weapons in order to be ready for battle. It takes daily use of spiritual weapons. Are you ready?

Armed and Dangerous (Part 4)

Ephesians 6: 10-13

Our final weapon, last but not least, is prayer. "And pray in the Spirit on all occasions with all kinds of prayers and requests... (vs 18)." Prayer is such a powerful weapon, and yet, it is one of the major weapons that we neglect. In this fast pace that drives us, do we take time to pray? Do we wait until the storm comes before we pray? But, I must encourage you to have a lifestyle of prayer, not a situational prayer life; meaning, that you only pray when things get difficult. "Be joyful always, pray continually." 1 Thessalonians 5: 17

Beloved we are in a spiritual battle. I'm just going to be real; the enemy does not like you or me, why? Because, we belong to Jesus, we are no longer on the enemy's side, therefore we are his enemy. Our weapon of prayer needs to be used regularly. Soldiers have to clean their weapons daily, they have to inspect it and use it daily. You've heard the old adage, "If you don't use it, you lose it". No, we are never lost from our Father, but our connection with Him will be compromised. Prayer is the channel to God the Father that keeps us connected and in communion with Him. Jesus said in John 15: 5, "I am the Vine; you are the branches. If a man remains in Me and I in him, he will bear much fruit; apart from Me you can do nothing." Prayer is communicating with the God of heaven. Deuteronomy 4: 7 ..."God is near us when we pray to Him." The bible says, that from inside the fish, Jonah prayed (Jonah 2: 1). In your tight, difficult situation... pray. Don't believe the lie from the enemy, that Lord doesn't hear you, He does hear your prayer and He cares.

Ambassadors

"We are therefore Christ's ambassadors, as though God were making His appeal through us. We implore you on Christ's behalf: Be reconciled to God." 2 Corinthians 5: 20

As we know, an ambassador is a high ranking official that represents a country to another country. In this position, the ambassador assumes various roles assisting the government, and members of the nation to fulfill their needs, as well as, acts as a liaison between the countries. Did you know that we are ambassadors...Christ's ambassadors? We represent Him everywhere that we go. We carry the honor and highest credential that of being a child of God. In that perspective, how are you measuring up? Are trials and issues causing you to lose focus? Remember, they are only tests...tests to strengthen you, and to grow you up.

When life throws a fast ball of problems at you do you throw that same ball back at others angrily, impatiently, or lovingly? If we're not careful, the enemy can deceive us by keeping us focused on the problems and in turn, cause us to act in such ways that don't reflect the glory or sovereignty of God.

In practical terms, if something happens on your job that irritates you and you take that attitude with you to lunch, in traffic on the way home, then to the store, and finally home. Can God get any glory in that? No. Guess what has happened? The enemy has checked one thing off his list and said, "I got her again." Beloved, let's not give the enemy an inch, and definitely not a foothold. Stand tall and strong for the Lord in your walk, because someone is watching and it could very well be the person that God has put on assignment for you. Something to think about...

A Vessel to Be Used

You do not delight in sacrifice, or I would bring it; you do not take pleasure in burnt offerings. The sacrifices of God are a broken spirit; a broken and contrite heart, O God, you will not despise. Psalm 51: 16-17

In the world anything that is broken beyond repairing is tossed out-discarded. It is viewed as junk. In my spare time, I love to frequent antique, consignment, and thrift stores. Why, because there is always something that someone has given or thrown away that in their eyes is no longer useful. In this text, David is broken and some may view as beyond repairing, because of the sin he committed against God-adultery and murder.

In Romans 6: 23 it says, "For the wages of sin is death, but the gift of God is eternal life in Christ Jesus our Lord." When we sin something dies; there are consequences we must face for our sin. If a person commits murder, though he repents, he will still have to go to jail. In David's case, a man was murdered, and his first child died (2 Samuel 12: 19). David repented; he was broken before God, and God forgave him.

Beloved, God will not despise a broken spirit and a contrite heart. If you are playing around with sin and have not confessed and repented, do it now. If you have taken up residency with being comfortable in your sin, repent now. We've all heard the old adage, "one man's trash is another man's treasure," so it is with us. Although, David had many family trials as a consequence of his sin, he lived to accomplish great things for God and is still today known as a man after God's own heart. God will take our trash, our broken unusable jars of clay and use it for His glory.

A Plan of Redemption

"And I will put enmity between you and the woman, and between your offspring and hers; He will crush your head, and you will strike His heel." Genesis 3: 15

After the fall of man, God had a redeeming plan to save mankind. Through one man's disobedience came a plan of redeeming grace and love through one Man, our Lord Jesus Christ with only one condition of accepting His free gift of salvation.

The prophets prophesied that He would come thousands of years before, and the irony of this amazing story is that though His people, the Jews, were anticipating the coming of the Messiah, they did not recognize Him nor did they receive Him.

Beloved, do you recognize Jesus when He shows up in your life? Maybe, He doesn't show up the way we want Him to, but He does show up. I pray that we remember Him like never before, and live a life of consecration and peace just thanking Him for first the gift of salvation, and secondly to be in expectation of His coming and showing up in our lives in whatever way He deems sufficient.

"See, my Servant will act wisely; He will be raised and lifted up and highly exalted." Isaiah 52: 13

A New Day Has Come

For to us a child is born, to us a Son is given, and the government will be on His shoulders. And He will be called Wonderful Counselor, Prince of Peace. Isaiah 9: 6

Oh...the days of anticipation, wondering...what will I get for Christmas? Hoping...I get that bike, that tape recorder (now I'm dating myself), or that easy bake oven. I still remember the colored wheel shining its light on our silver sparkling Christmas tree changing the colors to red, green and blue, Christmas music playing, the coffee table filled with bowls of nuts and fruit, and watching the snow fall. *It was beginning to look like Christmas* at the Brown house, mama, my three brothers and me. We may not have had a lot, but we had each other and this was our Christmas.

Children have an unbreakable faith and belief; their hope is refreshing and relentless, a kind of belief that we all can learn from. Like children with an endless hope, Israel too had hope and longed for the Savior in spite of their repeated cycle of disobedience and repentance from one generation to the next. But, God had a plan and He sent the prophet Isaiah to tell the people about God's plan of Salvation through the Messiah.

Beloved, that day has already come...the Messiah has come and He will return again, that is our hope and it should be our anticipation. Be in expectation everyday of the Savior's return; He will settle every account. Though the world may look bleak God has a plan. Keep your spirit hopeful, and encouraged of what He will do in and through your life and the life that is to come. *"May the God of hope fill you with all joy and peace as you trust Him, so that you may overflow with hope by the power of the Holy Spirit." Romans 15: 13*

A Message of Love

"For I am convinced that neither death nor life, neither angels nor demons, neither the present nor the future, nor any powers, neither height nor depth, nor anything else in all creation, will be able to separate us from the love of God that is in Christ Jesus our Lord." Romans 8: 38-39

I love reminders or those little notes that I write to myself such as sticky notes, notes saved in my computer, notes on my phone, and of course, my calendar. These notes are valuable to me, because they keep me on task and very organized. However, when I don't rely on these reminders, at times, I forget something that was on my 'to do list.' Reminders are important simply because they direct the mind to points of reference.

Beloved, those times that you feel guilty or you doubt God's love for you, refer to those mental notes about God's love for you and make it personal. Go back to the place where you first learned of His love and live there; don't move. It doesn't matter what you've done; His love is not predicated on your past, present, and your future.

Keep those mental reminders of His love for you at all times. Don't associate His love with earthly or fleshly love, and don't compare or identify His love to the same kind of love that you experience. God's love is beyond our understanding. *"For God so loved the world that He gave His one and only Son, that whoever believes in Him shall not perish but have eternal life." John 3: 16*

A Message of Hope

"But now I urge you to keep up your courage, because not one of you will be lost; only the ship will be destroyed." Acts 27: 22

Paul had warned the men about their disastrous voyage and their possible loss (27:10), but instead of taking heed to his advice, the centurion gave the order to proceed. How often do we ignore warning signs, an abnormal headache or back pain, the engine light, a yield sign in traffic? How many times have you told your son or daughter, "Do this or that?"

How often has the Lord said to us to turn right and instead we turned left? Let me be the first to admit how I have held on to the reigns too long and did not listen to the voice of God. It is often the insatiable urge to be totally in control, or the false assurance that we are always one step ahead of the warning; as if we have it all together, and at any moment can pull it all together. These men had the determination to sail in spite of Paul's warning, which almost cost them their lives.

Beloved, if you have found yourself in the center of a raging storm that may seem as powerful as a hurricane, possibly because of not heeding to the warning signs, or if your child has gone astray, don't lose hope. Hang in there and weather the storm. God will not forsake you. He has not forgotten you. It doesn't matter if you caused the storm, or you just happened to get thrown aboard the ship in the midst of the storm, keep your hope in God and hang onto Him, your Anchor. Remember all of His promises, stand on the word, and do not lose your hope.

31 Flavors

"I am not ashamed of the gospel, because it is the power of God for the salvation of everyone who believes: first for the Jew, then for the Gentile." Romans 1: 16

Out of all the flavors to choose from at the ice cream parlor what do you choose, chocolate, vanilla, strawberry, or my favorite, butter pecan? "Oh, what do I want?" This is the question that I ask myself every time that I stand in front of the ice cream counter (not often); decisions, decisions, decisions. So it is with our lives with so much in the world to choose from, immorality and compromise have taken center stage.

The enemy has deceived main stream media, everything goes...says who, God? I don't think so. God is the same yesterday, today, and forever (Hebrews 13:8). He changes not; don't get drawn into what society deems as the standard. God is still sovereign and the bible is still the only standard for our lives. Stand for truth and stand for righteousness.

Beloved, what will you choose compromise or holiness and righteousness? Something to think about...

He Got Up!

"On the first day of the week, very early in the morning, the women took the spices they had prepared and went to the tomb. They found the stone rolled away from the tomb, but when they entered, they did not find the body of the Lord Jesus. While they were wondering about this, suddenly two men in clothes that gleamed like lightning stood beside them. In their fright the women bowed down with their faces to the ground, but the men said to them. "Why do you look for the living among the dead? He is not here; He has risen! Remember, how He told you, while He was still with you in Galilee?" Luke 24: 1-7

Of the three and a half years of Jesus' ministry spent with the disciples, He told them several times that He would be leaving them. The Jews knew of Jesus' statement, "Destroy this temple, and I will raise it again in three days." (John 2: 19) Of course, during those times they did not understand what He meant, and the disciples did not want Him to leave. Once He was crucified, they did not know what to do next. It is the same way with us. The Lord has been with some of us a long time. He has given us "everything pertaining to life (2 Peter 1: 3). Yet, we are challenged with what to do next.

Beloved, my challenge to you is…get up. That's what He did. He got up! Hallelujah! Thank you Jesus, He got up! He has risen! He did not stay in the grave. His purpose, His assignment was to get up, to live, so that we can live and spend eternity with Him and to live abundantly on earth. Jesus said, "The thief comes to steal, kill, and destroy," I have come that they may have life and have it to the full." John 10: 10. If you, like the disciples, are wondering what to do next, get up. You have resurrection power living in you; anything living should be moving.

www.ingramcontent.com/pod-product-compliance
Lightning Source LLC
LaVergne TN
LVHW051812080426
835513LV00017B/1920